Brilliant As The Sun

A retelling of Srimad Bhagavatam
'The Beautiful Science of God'

Canto One

The Sages of Naimisharanya

by

Krishna Dharma
and
Chintamani Dhama Dasi

DEDICATION

This book is dedicated to our spiritual teacher and guide, His Divine Grace A.C. Bhaktivedanta Swami Prabhupada, whose epic translation of *Srimad Bhagavatam*, complete with elaborate commentary, provided the basis for this work. We offer him our sincerest respects and pray that he will be pleased with our humble offering.

CONTENTS

"Simply by hearing the Vedic literature, Srimad Bhagavatam, one can have direct connection with the Supreme Personality of Godhead, Lord Krishna, and thereby attain the highest perfection of life by transcending worldly miseries, illusion and fearfulness. Srimad Bhagavatam is so made that one becomes at once engaged in the path of self-realization by hearing the topics... Although it is especially meant for the paramahamsas, or those totally engaged in self-realization, it works into the depths of the hearts of worldly men. Such persons are engaged in sense gratification, but even they will find in this Vedic literature a remedial measure for their material condition." ~Srila Prabhupada

INTRODUCTION

The ancient Vedic texts describe four great ages of man that repeat themselves in an endless cycle. Beginning with a 'golden age', known as Satya Yuga, they gradually degrade until the final age, which is known as Kali Yuga, the 'iron age' of quarrel and hypocrisy. Five thousand years ago, when Kali Yuga began, the great sage Vyasadeva saw in a mystical vision the terrible miseries we would endure during this age. Out of compassion, he sent us the transcendental teaching known as *Srimad Bhagavatam*, which literally means 'the beautiful pastimes of the Supreme Lord and his pure devotees'. This great spiritual treatise contains the secrets by which we can free ourselves from suffering and experience ever-increasing joy.

The *Bhagavatam's* mysteries remained locked up in the Sanskrit language until recent times, when His Divine Grace A.C. Bhaktivedanta Swami (Srila) Prabhupada translated it into English and provided his own scholarly commentaries. At an advanced age, he personally brought these teachings to all parts of the world. We are deeply indebted to him, for his writings have transformed our lives. Thus, we are moved to share the *Bhagavatam's* profound messages. There is mounting upheaval, fear and uncertainty in today's world. The *Bhagavatam* teaches us how to become like a lotus flower which, although sitting in a muddy lake, is untouched by the waters. We hope by reading and meditating on the *Bhagavatam's* profound wisdom, you will gradually become fearless, and experience joy in your hearts, despite your external circumstances.

The lessons of *Srimad Bhagavatam* are in the form of discussions between sages, gods, kings and great saints, and are delivered against the backdrop of historical events. For the most part, the original text only briefly touches on the details of these long passed incidents, focusing instead on the *Bhagavatam's* philosophical instructions. In this retelling we have dramatised the historical incidents surrounding the conversations but have carefully kept the core teachings intact.

First time readers, unfamiliar with the spiritual concepts presented here, may feel the need to skip over some of the more challenging philosophical sections. We have thus written abstracts at the start of each chapter so you may quickly grasp the essential points. For those readers who wish to study the original *Srimad Bhagavatam*, we have also included chapter and verse numbers to enable easy cross reference to that text. In many places, we have inserted questions not found in the original text. This is to help the reader see the flow of the conversations. Often these questions have been borrowed from the commentaries of Vishvanatha Chakravarti Thakur, a great saint and commentator on *Srimad Bhagavatam*.

We have also included a table as an appendix, showing how the conversations and stories are nestled within other conversations.

The *Bhagavatam* is comprised of twelve cantos or divisions. This book is a rendition of the first canto, which introduces the *Bhagavatam's* foundational conversation between Suta Goswami and an assembly of sages at Naimisharanya, a holy site still found in India. The first nine cantos reveal God's power and greatness, while the tenth and eleventh cantos show his sweetness and charming personality. The twelfth canto ends the work with a description of the dreadful ills that will unfold during the 432,000 years of the Kali Yuga. We will gradually present all twelve cantos in serial form.

It is advised that one hear *Srimad Bhagavatam* from self-realised devotees of Krishna. Since we are not such persons, one might ask why we undertook this work. The primary reason is the order of Srila Prabhupada, who asked that his followers present his works to others in their own words. Indeed, he sometimes had his disciples give lectures on the *Bhagavatam* in his own presence, knowing that this is one of the best ways to assimilate its instructions. The key requirement is that one adhere closely to the teachings of the self-realised souls, and not try to exceed them by the power of one's limited intellect. We have rigorously endeavoured to abide by this edict, always carefully referring to Srila Prabhupada's translation and commentaries. We hope, therefore, that our humble attempt will attract the reader to subsequently take up the study of his work, for he has shown himself to be without doubt the qualified teacher of the *Bhagavatam*.

We pray our efforts to share *Srimad Bhagavatam* will please its author, the divine incarnation Vyasadeva, as well as our beloved teacher Srila Prabhupada, and all the Lord's pure devotees. We offer them our most sincere respects and beg that they bless us by empowering this book to play some small part in uplifting those suffering in this awful age.

Om Tat Sat

Krishna Dharma

Chintamani Dhama Dasi

INVOCATION

(1)

To you the all-pervading Lord, I offer all esteem.
From whom the worlds originate, on whom they do depend,
which seeming real to gods and men, are but passing dreams,
that you bring back into yourself, when time comes to its end.
Supreme Godhead, who taught Brahma, cosmic creator.
Nothing is unknown to you, nor can it ever be,
for all existence must but move according to your law.
On you my mind does always dwell, who dwells eternally,
above illusion's sway; the one reality.

(2)

This beautiful Bhagavata does the highest truth contain;
devoid of all deception, to free us from all pain.
Only known by those who are released from matter's thrall,
destroying delusion for the benefit of all.
Compiled by Sage Vyasadeva, it will reveal the Lord,
to any who with faith do read its transcendental words.

(3)

Men of wisdom and of taste, please relish this fine fruit,
of the wish-fulfilling tree of ancient Vedic lore.
Made sweeter still by the lips of Shuka, sage astute;
it does bestow on all a bliss that lasts forevermore.

1. Questions by The Sages

At the dawn of the dark age known as Kali Yuga, a great concourse of sages assemble at the holy site of Naimisharanya. They question the saintly Suta Goswami as to the best means of propitiating the Supreme Lord to ameliorate the evils of the impending age. Suta has just returned from a lengthy pilgrimage, during which he heard a profound spiritual discourse from the erudite mystic, Shukadeva Goswami. The sages ask Suta six questions:

1. What is most beneficial for humanity?
2. What are the essential duties given in the Vedas?
3. Why does Krishna appear as the son of Vasudeva and Devaki?
4. Describe Krishna's pastimes.
5. Describe the pastimes of Krishna's other incarnations (including that of creation).
6. In whom did religious principles take shelter after Krishna left this world?

(1:4-5) "Om, *svaha, svaha, svaha!*" The crackling of the sacrificial fires as priests fed them with ladles of ghee was drowned out by the sages' loud chanting of sacred incantations. As the sun rose over Naimisharanya Forest, the priests manning the fires exchanged places with those reciting the mantras. Blackened by the smoke, they went to the nearby river to bathe.

The elderly Shaunaka, son of the celestial sage Bhrigu, walked from one fire to another, checking with the chief priests to ensure they had all they needed to continue their sacrifice. "Bring more firewood here!" he called out to the runners.

As he turned toward the next fire, a young brahmin hurried toward him. "O holy one, the revered Suta Goswami has returned!"

Shaunaka's eyes widened in happiness. "Suta is back? Where is he?"

"Bathing in the river, my lord. I just came from there."

Shaunaka immediately assembled a greeting party. As they walked to the river, they chanted prayers glorifying the spiritual master. In the early morning light, they saw the elderly Suta, still wet from his bath, walking toward them, smiling broadly and holding his water pot and mendicant's staff. Shaunaka and the welcoming party bowed down on the soft sand in obeisance, and Suta returned their respects. Rising, they tightly embraced.

"Welcome back, dear Suta," said Shaunaka. "We have missed you."

The two friends walked side by side surrounded by the others who continued to chant. When they arrived at the sacrificial fires, Suta sat upon a straw mat and the sages, eager to hear his news, surrounded him.

"Dear brahmins," began Suta, "I congratulate you on your dedication to your service here. For a long time, you have maintained this great sacrifice to supplicate the Supreme Lord. Your mission is crucial for the world's good."

"Thank you Suta," said Shaunaka. "Still, we are haunted by the doubt that our efforts may not be enough."

Suta looked at the disheartened sages with compassion. "In that respect, I have good news. After travelling far and wide, by the Lord's grace, I had the good fortune to hear from Vyasadeva's exalted son, Shukadeva Goswami."

Some sages called out, "What did you learn from him? Pray tell us."

"Did he say anything about the poor souls suffering in the dark age of Kali?" Shaunaka asked anxiously.

Suta nodded sadly. "Yes, he described in some detail the abominable conditions of this age. Animals will be slaughtered mercilessly. Children, women and the elderly will be neglected and abused. Neighbour will cheat neighbour. The earth's fertility will gradually reduce and there will be no rain. Rice, wheat, milk, sugar and other staple foods will eventually disappear. At the end of Kali Yuga, if a person lives for twenty to thirty years, he will be considered an old man. People will be foolish; easily cheated by false religious teachers. They will be persecuted and overtaxed by the government; so much so that, giving up hearth and home, they will run to the forest and hills in disappointment and confusion. In the end, mothers and fathers will consume their own children."[1]

As he spoke, Shaunaka's and the other sages' faces contorted with sorrow. "This is worse than we imagined," said Shaunaka. "I fear our sacrifices will not be sufficient."

Suta reassured the sages. "My dear friends, be peaceful at heart. Shukadeva also taught the most effective method for countering these evils."

"Where did you meet the illustrious Shukadeva?" asked Shaunaka.

Suta's countenance became grave. "My dear brothers, I met him on the banks of the holy River Ganges near Hastinapura. He had arrived there to assist the emperor of the world, King Parikit, to prepare for his death."

A great wail of disbelief arose from the assembly. The mighty Parikit dead? How? Many called out asking Suta to explain. Shaunaka raised his hands to quieten the assembly.

"Be patient. Suta has travelled for many months. He is tired. We can question him more after he is rested and refreshed."

It was decided that the next morning Suta would address the sages. That evening some of the younger men constructed an elevated seat on a small mound in the centre of the sacrificial arena. Everyone wanted to hear Suta speak. The sages decided to simply keep the fires burning, but to suspend the rituals. "We need not chant mantras," said Shaunaka. "Suta's discourse will be sufficient."

Another sage said, "Brothers, let us appoint one amongst us to speak on behalf of us all. We can confer with him. Otherwise, if everyone is constantly calling out questions, Suta will find it hard to speak."

Shaunaka was elected to pose their questions. For several hours he sat in conference with other senior sages to determine what questions he should put to Suta. The next morning Suta took his seat with due ceremony, and Shaunaka sat on a platform a little below him. The other sages sat in a great semi-circle around the two friends.

(1:6-8) Shaunaka commenced the proceedings. "Dear Suta Goswami, you are the eldest and wisest amongst us all. You have thoroughly studied and taught the Puranas, the *Mahabharata* and all the scriptures describing religious duties. You are acquainted with the teachings of the great Vyasadeva, the Lord's literary incarnation, and you have heard from other erudite sages. Surely, they have bestowed upon you all knowledge, due to your gentle and submissive nature. Pray tell us what you have scientifically learned from them."

Suta bowed his head. He was hardly worthy of the sages' plaudits. He was a mere messenger whose duty was to pass on the teachings of his great master without adulteration. Folding his palms, he said, "I shall tell you everything I have learned."

"Dear Suta," said Shaunaka, "you have travelled for years and have surely heard much. It would take much time for you to repeat it all. We have therefore prepared six questions which we would like you to answer."

"Very well then, please ask."

(1:9) Shaunaka folded his palms. "As you know, we have gathered here to perform a thousand year sacrifice to benefit the people of Kali Yuga. Initially, we wanted to improve their material happiness by propitiating the gods. However, after hearing from your late father, Romaharshana, we learned that such happiness automatically follows spiritual advancement. Please, therefore, tell us in a simplified and concise manner what you have ascertained to be the ultimate spiritual good for all people. Is there some

5

way the ordinary man can easily become free from misery and achieve eternal happiness?"

(1:10) Suta smiled. "You are all intelligent sages. Let me explain to you the various spiritual attainments one might seek, and you can decide which is best."

Shaunaka shook his head. "There is confusion on this point, and these are difficult times. No one will live long enough to make an extensive study of scripture in order to determine life's highest aim. Even if they do have a sufficient lifespan, they have no inclination to study. Of those who might try, very few have the intelligence to understand, and they will not have access to learned persons who can help them. Even with such association, they are likely to be afflicted by bodily and mental woes that will obstruct them from serious spiritual enquiry. If somehow, they do manage to make such an attempt, they may still come to the wrong conclusion. Please, therefore, give us a clear answer."

"Very well," said Suta. "I will try my best to respond. What is your second question?"

(1:11) Shaunaka continued. "We would like to know the best means for attaining life's goal. There are numerous scriptures describing countless duties. It takes many years to properly understand and apply all these injunctions. Please tell us which of them are essential and will benefit everyone in all circumstances."

(1:12-13,20) Suta's eyes expanded and his face lit up with a broad smile. These were perfect questions aimed at attaining life's greatest good, not just some temporary benefit soon lost in the course of time.

"Thank you, dear Shaunaka, your enquiries are most enlivening. What else do you wish to know?"

"O Suta, you are truly blessed, for you know the reason for Krishna's appearance as the son of

Vasudeva and Devaki. It is hard to understand why he and his divine brother, Balarama, performed so many human-like pastimes, such as playing like young children and dancing with the *gopis*. These activities are so different from those of other avatars. Please explain his purpose as you have heard it from the great masters, for we feel sure this will benefit everyone."

(1:14-15) As he spoke about Krishna, Shaunaka's mind became infused with spiritual happiness. "Surely there is something wonderful about Krishna's appearance." Then in a more serious tone he added, "Living beings who are entangled in the complicated meshes of birth and death can be freed immediately by even unconsciously chanting his holy name, which drives away the fear of death. Indeed, we have also heard that Krishna's power is such that those who surrender to him can liberate anyone. Such devotees are said to be more purifying than the sacred Ganges, for simply by seeing them, one benefits. Therefore, it seems to us that by understanding the mystery of Krishna's appearance and activities, we can better aid the people of Kali Yuga."

(1:16-18) "Your deduction is most intelligent," said Suta. "Krishna's pastimes are indeed significant. What are your other questions?"

"The Supreme Lord's acts are so magnificent and gracious that great liberated saints like Narada sing of them. Please, therefore, describe Krishna's glorious activities. Who is that person, desiring liberation from the miseries of the Kali Age, who would not want to hear about them? Please also describe the pastimes of other incarnations, including those of universal creation, maintenance and destruction. All the Lord's activities are transcendental and auspicious."

(1:19) Lifting the corner of his mouth in an amused smile, Suta replied, "This will take much time. Krishna performs unlimited pastimes and his avatars are countless."

"Even so," said Shaunaka, "we are greatly curious to hear these topics. Please explain whatever you feel you can."

Turning to the assembled sages for confirmation, he continued, "I think all of us would agree that this is time well spent. Indeed, spiritually advanced souls relish such talks constantly."

(1:21-22) The others cheered loudly expressing their agreement with Shaunaka. Suta's eyes twinkled mischievously. "I am a little surprised that great brahmins like yourselves, absorbed in ritualistic sacrifices, should be so enthusiastic to hear about the Lord."

Shaunaka looked over at the fires and then turned back to Suta with a solemn expression. "We already knew the Age of Kali has commenced, but after what you told us yesterday, we have become aware of just how much degradation and suffering it will bring. We have lost interest in our sacrifice, doubting its efficacy, and we only want to hear from you about Krishna. We therefore thank Providence for sending you to guide us safely to the other side of this terrible age."

(1:23) Suta praised Shaunaka and the sages for their thoughtful enquiries and humbly replied, "I am merely the Lord's instrument, conveying his messages. Please let me know your sixth and final question."

"When Lord Krishna was personally present, he protected religious principles. Now that he has departed, how will they be preserved?"

A flock of birds flew into the sky from a blossoming branch, sending down a shower of flower petals. The birds' cries mixed with the calls of peacocks sounding from the forest, as Suta began to speak.

2. Attaining Divinity

After hearing the sages' six questions, in this chapter Suta answers the first two questions. He explains that life's highest attainment is to develop our loving relationship with Krishna; and that life's most essential duties are to continuously hear about, glorify, remember and worship Krishna.

(2:1-4) As was his custom, Suta recited prayers petitioning divine mercy.

"I bow down to Shukadeva Goswami, who left home while still a boy. For the welfare of all people, he later spoke *Srimad Bhagavatam,* the beautiful science of God, to Emperor Parikit."

The sages raised their arms and called out, "Glories to Shukadeva Goswami!"

With closed eyes, Suta spoke in prayerful tones. "Before reciting *Srimad Bhagavatam,* which destroys all ignorance, I pay obeisance to its compiler, Sage Vyasadeva, and to its patron deities, the divine incarnations Nara and Narayana. Obeisance also to the

Goddess of Learning, Sarasvati, and to the subject of the work, Lord Krishna."

(2:5) Again and again, the assembled sages raised their arms and joyfully echoed Suta's invocation with cries of, "Jaya! Jaya!"

Suta waited patiently until his excited audience settled. He first praised their intelligent enquiries. "By asking such questions, you have rendered humanity a great service. Since your questions relate to Lord Krishna, the answers will satisfy everyone's heart."

(2:6) Suta looked out at the sages. "Let us start with your first two questions. Our most important duties are those which awaken our love for Krishna. This love, which is life's highest goal, is called *prema bhakti*. Only when our devotional service becomes spontaneous, unmotivated and uninterrupted will we feel completely satisfied."

Shaunaka rubbed his chin. This was a surprise. The Vedas spoke of dharma, *artha*, *kama* and *moksha* as life's great aims[1]. How is it Suta had not mentioned any of these?

He said, "Bhakti?" Is that not for sentimentalists unable to perform the high-grade activities of karma, *jnana* or *ashtanga* yogas?"[2]

(2:7) Suta said, "Both qualified and unqualified people can serve Krishna. By executing *bhakti* yoga[3] anyone can automatically achieve transcendental knowledge and detachment from material life; goals difficult to achieve on other spiritual paths."

"It seems bhakti yoga is both easy and sublime," said Shaunaka.

Suta smiled. "Certainly. It is sublime for pure devotees serious to connect with Krishna and it is easy for neophytes on the threshold of devotion. After all, the Supreme Lord welcomes all living beings, even those who are without any worldly status."

Shaunaka said, "The Vedas frequently speak of *varnashrama dharma*.[4] Are these duties important?"

(2:8) Suta replied, "*Varnashrama* duties are helpful as they promote social cooperation so that everyone has time to hear about Krishna, which is the main *dharma*.[5] This awakens our attraction to him and thus our taste for hearing about him increases.[6] Attraction for Krishna should be our only goal. If by performing *varnasharma* duties, we do not increase our taste for hearing about and glorifying Krishna we are simply wasting our time.[7]

Shaunaka said, "Is there *any* value in material success or liberation?"

(2:9) "Real liberation is *prema bhakti*.[8] *Varnashrama* duties and their results are meant to help us attain this goal alone.[9] Material gains achieved by one's worldly work should not be used to unnecessarily increase material enjoyment.[10]

(2:10) "No one should waste their life pursuing sense pleasure. We need only enough material facilities to keep the body healthy and the mind peaceful. An intelligent person focuses on realising the Absolute Truth, as this is only possible in human life. We should not become distracted by bodily enjoyment which is available even to animals."

"What do you mean by 'the Absolute Truth'?" asked Shaunaka.

(2:11) Suta said, "According to one's consciousness the Absolute Truth is perceived either as Brahman, Paramatma or Bhagavan. Brahman is all-pervasive spiritual energy, the basis of material and spiritual existence. Brahman realisation, which is described extensively in the Upanishads, is the first stage of spiritual realisation. Since Brahman is energy it must have an energetic source. This source is Paramatma, the all-pervading, localised aspect of God. He can be seen by advanced yogis within everyone's heart and also in every atom of material existence. The highest realisation of the Absolute Truth, however, is Bhagavan, the Personality of Godhead, who exhibits the supreme opulence of loving pastimes with his intimate associates. When the devotee attains *prema*, he realises Bhagavan and is able to participate in his sublime pastimes. All three phases of realisation are of the same Absolute Truth."

"How can one truth be seen in three different ways?" asked Shaunaka.

"Consider this example," replied Suta. He pointed to the light shining through the tree branches. "Sunshine is like Brahman. Just as lower life forms only perceive the sunshine not the sun, the least qualified transcendentalists only perceive Brahman. We humans, however, also perceive the sun globe which is the source of the rays. This higher knowledge is like realising the Supersoul. A person with celestial vision can see the sun god himself and this is like realising the Personality of Godhead, Bhagavan. All three are aspects of the same sun, but what one sees depends on how evolved his consciousness is."

"How can we realise the Absolute Truth?"

(2:12) "Anyone serious to know the Absolute Truth can do so by hearing the Vedas from a self realised person.[11] By acting on these teachings we realise the difference between matter and spirit. Such knowledge evokes material detachment, and as we continue to hear and apply the knowledge, we will gradually perceive all three features of the Absolute.

(2:13) "However, we can only perceive the Absolute Truth to the degree he reveals himself to

13

us.[12] Therefore, the real purpose of *varnashrama* duties is to enable us to cooperate for his satisfaction.

(2:14) "No matter what our *varnashrama* position is, whether we are a brahmin or a *shudra*, to please Krishna everyone must engage in the essential activities of devotion, hearing about, glorifying, remembering and worshiping him with focused attention. These activities, known as *sadhana bhakti*,[13] please Krishna who then personally protects us from the reactions of our sinful activities.[14]

(2:15) "We can cut through the complex tangle of karmic reactions simply by remembering Krishna. Such remembrance is only possible if we hear about him."

Suta looked around the assembly. There was an urgency in his voice as he asked, "How can anyone who understands this truth neglect to hear Krishna's teachings?"

Shaunaka sighed. "Unfortunately, hardly anyone has faith in *bhakti yoga*. Most people are attracted to Vedic rituals for material advancement, or to austerity and meditation to attain liberation. How will this change?"

(2.16) Suta thought for a moment and then said, "O brahmins! The first requirement is to receive the causeless mercy of an advanced devotee. Such devotees are very dear to Krishna because they take great risks to propagate his glories. Krishna bestows his mercy on anyone who serves them.[15] By Krishna's mercy one gets faith in him and the process of *bhakti*. This faith gradually matures into an attraction for hearing about him.

(2.17) "As the Supersoul within, Krishna cleanses material desires from the hearts of the unpretentious who hear about him with even a little

faith. Just by respectfully and attentively hearing about and glorifying Krishna one increases in virtue.[16]
Appendix 1

(2:18) "If one is fortunate enough to hear the science of God known as the *Srimad Bhagavatam* from someone who fully understands and lives that science, his taste for hearing it increases. He then determinedly hears *Bhagavatam* daily and always serves advanced devotees. At this stage of steady devotional service all the contamination in his heart is almost destroyed. *Appendix 2*

(2.19) "The first sign of steady devotional service is that we are freed of anger, greed, or any other influence of the modes of passion and ignorance.[17]

We will relish hearing about, glorifying, remembering and worshiping Krishna when we lose our attraction for material enjoyment.[18] By continuing with our devotional practices, we eventually revive our pure spiritual nature. This is variously known as *shuddha-sattva*, *brahma-bhuta*,[19] and *ashakti*,[20] At this stage the devotee harms no one and is always happy because he sees Krishna in everyone's heart.

(2.20) "When the satisfaction experienced by one's devotional practices further intensifies it is known as *bhava*.[21] This matures into *prema*, divine love, at which time the devotee personally experiences Krishna's form, qualities, pastimes, powers and sweetness.[22] *Appendix 3*

(2.21) "Then the knot of false ego is cut by Krishna, releasing the spirit soul from his entanglement with matter. At that time the devotee has no more doubts for he sees his own spiritual identity in relation to Krishna."[23]

The assembly sat in complete silence. Suta had

succinctly described how one could achieve life's highest perfection without any need for difficult yoga practises and severe austerities. It was so simple, just hear about and glorify Krishna. Who could not do that? After a few moments Shaunaka said, "Wonderful, my dear Suta. Bhakti-yoga is so sublime."

(2.22) Suta said, "Therefore, from time immemorial discerning transcendentalists have practised devotional service to Krishna because it bestows the highest result and is easy and joyful to perform."

Shaunaka and the sages listened attentively. When Suta stopped speaking, there was a brief silence and then Shaunaka said, "Brahma, Vishnu and Shiva are all considered divine incarnations. Does their worship also bestow *prema bhakti*?"

(2.23) "They are known as *Guna Avatars*," replied Suta. "Krishna does not directly contact the material energy. To create the universe, he incarnates through the mode of passion as Brahma; to maintain it, he incarnates through goodness as Vishnu; and to destroy it he incarnates through ignorance as Shiva. Of these three, only Vishnu worship bestows ultimate benefit."

Shaunaka said, "Do you mean we can attain *prema bhakti* by worshipping Vishnu, but not by worshipping Brahma and Shiva?"

"That's correct."

"Since all three are Krishna's Guna Avatars, why is not the worship of Brahma and Shiva as beneficial as the worship of Vishnu," asked Shaunaka.

(2.24) Suta pointed to a nearby sacrificial fire. "Observe this fire," he said, "when the flames are blazing it is easy to see."

All the sages turned to look at the incandescent flames leaping brightly into the morning

16

sky. When, however, on Suta's request the priests placed more kindling on the fires, the flames became smothered. Remarking on this, Suta said, "As we know, the fire is still present under that wood. Nevertheless, because of the preponderance of fuel, the fire is hidden."

As they kept watching the sacrificial pits, smoke billowed out from the newly stoked fires filling the early morning sky.

Suta continued, "Smoke is also an integral part of fire, but when predominant it too conceals the flames. Nevertheless, smoke is a better indicator of the presence of fire than wood."

The sages looked quizzically back and forth from the smoky sacrificial fires to Suta. What had fire, wood and smoke to do with Vishnu, Shiva and Brahma?

Suta continued. "Just as the sacrificial fire manifests as flames, wood and smoke, similarly the Supreme Lord manifests in this world as Vishnu, Shiva and Brahma. Vishnu, who governs the mode of goodness, is comparable to the flames. As flames are the essence of fire, similarly Vishnu is the spiritual form of the Lord and should therefore be worshipped.

"Shiva governs the mode of ignorance and is comparable to wood. Similarly, Brahma, who governs the mode of passion, is compared to smoke. As wood and smoke obscure the flames, similarly, worship of these two gods, governing the modes of passion and ignorance, obstructs spiritual realization.

(2:25) "In bygone days, great sages were primarily interested in attaining *prema bhakti*. Therefore, they only worshipped Vishnu or other incarnations of Krishna who are transcendental to material nature. Whoever follows their example will automatically attain liberation."

Shaunaka said, "If someone desires liberation would they not need to perform the various Vedic sacrifices worshipping the administrative gods? Surely one who fails to respect the gods by neglecting their worship cannot expect any good."

(2:26) "Those seriously intent on liberation should certainly show respect to the gods, even the frightful ones such as Goddess Kali. However, we should only worship Krishna or his integrated plenary portions, or *Vishnu-tattva* expansions."

"Can you explain?" asked Shaunaka.

Suta described how Krishna expands himself in two categories: *Vishnu-tattva*, and separated parts and parcels. The first category are divine avatars. They include Vishnu, Kurma, Varaha, Vamana, Rama, and many other incarnations, all of whom are to be worshipped. The separated parts and parcels are the conditioned souls whose position it is to serve the avatars. This category includes the gods.

"Why then do the Vedas describe sacrifices to the gods?" asked Shaunaka.

(2:27) "These are meant for those controlled by passion and ignorance, who think life's aim is to enjoy sex, wealth, power and family life."

"It seems then that the Vedas mislead people about life's true goal," said Shaunaka.

(2:28-29) Suta replied, "Less intelligent people do not properly understand the Vedas which actually teach that sacrifice, duty, meditation, austerity, and cultivating knowledge should all aim to please Krishna.

(2:30-31) "This is because Krishna is the root of all existence and all the gods. Unlike the gods, he always remains in his transcendental position, unaffected by matter, even though he creates and maintains it."

Shaunaka said, "Since Krishna is transcendental, he must be beyond material perception. How then can we know him?"

(2:32) "When you develop divine consciousness, you will see him in everything, including the hearts of all living beings."

"How can we foster this consciousness?"

Suta again pointed at the nearby sacrificial fires. The *arani* wood which had earlier been heaped on to the fires, was now bursting into flames.

He said, "In the same way that fire is kindled from wood by another fire, similarly divine consciousness is awakened by hearing proper spiritual messages from a self-realised soul."

Everyone applauded Suta's answer. When the sages quietened, Shaunaka continued his questioning. "Since Krishna is disinterested in material enjoyment, why does he enter the material world?"

(2:33) "The small spirit souls are unable to independently control or enjoy matter," replied Suta, "therefore Vishnu enters their hearts to act as the witness of their activities and desires, and also to enable them to gratify their senses as much as they merit. This is the Lord's kindness."

(2:34) "Since Krishna is present in everyone's heart as the Supersoul," said Shaunaka, "why does he also appear in different incarnations?"

Suta said, "The role of the Supersoul is to maintain the cosmos. However, when he comes as different incarnations, he does so to reclaim the fallen souls."

3. Divine Incarnations

Suta lists the incarnations of Vishnu which appear in the current epoch. He explains why the universal form of God, known as the Virat Rupa, is not included in that list, and also describes how one can achieve self-realisation. He ends with a brief description of Srimad Bhagavatam. In doing so, he answers the sages' sixth question.

(3:1-5) "My dear Suta, please tell us more about the Lord's incarnations," said Shaunaka. We are keen to hear everything you know about his pastimes."

Suta replied, "The first incarnation, the Purusha Avatar, creates the cosmic manifestation. From him came Brahma, the master engineer of the universe."

Suta explained that although there is one Purusha Avatar, also called the Supersoul, he manifests in three stages. The first is Mahavishnu who lies in the Karana or Causal Ocean, the basis of creation. Each time he exhales, countless universes emanate from the pores of his transcendental body. When he again inhales, they re-enter him. Mahavishnu expands himself into each universe as

Garbhodakashayi Vishnu. Lying in the ocean at the bottom of the universal egg, he provides the ingredients for creation such as earth, water, fire, air, and other essential components. These are manifested along with Brahma. He expands again as Kshirodakashayi Vishnu, who enters every atom, as well as the hearts of all beings.

Suta continued, "It is said that all the planets in the universe lie on the extensive body of Garbhodakashayi Vishnu. Nevertheless, he is fully and eternally spiritual. Through him come the divine incarnations who descend into the material world. He is the source of the gods and all species of life. The Purusha Avatar is generally not perceivable. By the Lord's grace, his pure devotee may sometimes see him with his thousands of faces, decorated with shining helmets, and adorned with glowing earrings and garlands. Arjuna saw that form just before the Battle of Kurukshetra."

(3:6-7) Suta enumerated the Lord's other incarnations who come through the Purusha Avatar. "First were the four Kumara brothers, sons of Brahma, who followed a strict vow of celibacy and underwent severe austerities. Next came Varaha, the boar incarnation, who rescued the earth when it fell into the nether regions.

(3:8-9) "Third was the godly sage, Narada, who compiled expositions of the Vedas explaining *bhakti-yoga*. He was followed by Nara-Narayana, the twin ascetic sons of the great King Dharma, who live in Badarika Ashram in the Himalayas. Because they appeared as twins, they are considered a single incarnation.

(3:10-12) "They were followed by Lord Kapila, foremost among the Siddhas or perfect mystics. He taught the Sankhya system of philosophy, which frees one from material entanglement. Then came Dattatreya, who also expounded Sankhya philosophy, and after this there appeared Yajna, who occupied the post of the chief god, Indra.

(3:13-15) "The eighth incarnation was Lord Rishabha who taught the path of spiritual perfection to his one hundred sons. After this was Prithu, the ideal king, who made the earth productive and beautiful. Then came the fish incarnation, Matsya. Assuming an immense form, he saved Vaivasvata Manu, the leader of mankind, from the waters of inundation.

(3:16-17) "In his eleventh incarnation, the Lord became the great turtle Kurma, who assisted the gods and demons in churning the milk ocean to produce the nectar of immortality. After this appeared Dhanvantari, who brought the nectar and later taught Ayurveda. He was followed by the exquisitely beautiful female incarnation Mohini, who tricked the demons and thereby enabled the gods to drink the nectar of immortality.

(3:18-21) "The fierce lion-headed Nrishinga descended as the fourteenth incarnation. He tore open the chest of the invincible demon, Hiranyakashipu, just as a basket weaver splits reeds. Then there appeared Vamana, the dwarf incarnation, whose two steps incredibly spanned the entire universe, thereby winning it back from the demon king, Bali, for the sake of the gods. Next came Parasurama who annihilated the deviant rulers of the earth in twenty-one great battles. He was followed by Vyasa, who compiled the Vedas.

(3:22-23) "When the gods prayed for deliverance from the powerful Rakshasa monarch, Ravana, the Lord appeared in his eighteenth incarnation as Ramachandra. In the next two incarnations, the nineteenth and twentieth, he came as Balarama and Krishna, who relieved the earth of her burden of warmongering kings."

(3:24-25) "There are also two avatars yet to appear. The first is Buddha who will take birth in Gaya. Although not presenting himself as God, he will teach a philosophy which will convince the atheists to accept his authority.

"The final incarnation is Kalki, who comes at the twilight of Kali-yuga to kill the many degraded leaders who will cause great disturbances. He will thereby re-establish religion and usher in a new golden age."

(3:26) Immersed in thoughts of Krishna, Suta became stunned with ecstasy. After some moments, he said, "O sages! Know that Krishna's incarnations are unlimited, like rivulets flowing from an inexhaustible lake. They appear whenever the spiritually ignorant create disorder. His purpose is to protect the pious."

(3:27) Suta explained that since the sages, gods, universal leaders and the great Progenitors who populate the universe are all empowered by the Lord's divine potency, they are also considered avatars.

(3:28) Shaunaka said, "I thought Krishna was supreme. Why do you say that he, like the other avatars, comes from the Purusha Avatar, Garbhodakashayi Vishnu?"

Suta held up his hands. "Do not misunderstand. Although I included Krishna in this list of incarnations, you should know that he is their source. All divinities are either his direct or subsidiary parts. Krishna is the original Supreme Personality of Godhead. Everything comes from him, including Vishnu. Therefore to serve Krishna with love is life's ultimate goal."

(3:29) Suta stressed that only when our loving

service attitude toward Krishna is awakened can we get full and permanent relief from misery. "To achieve this we must carefully hear and discuss the mysteries of his appearances with faith, every morning and evening."

Shaunaka raised a doubt. "Dear Suta, why did you not include in your list of incarnations, the cosmic arrangement of the planets known as the Virat Rupa? Many sages meditate on this as the Lord's universal form."

(3:30) Suta replied, "The Virat Rupa is an imaginary conception meant to help neophyte worshippers who cannot accept God's spiritual form and personality. Since they can only think in material terms, they believe that if God has a form, it limits him. By meditating on the Virat Rupa, gradually they adjust to the idea that God is a person. Shukadeva also described this meditation to Parikit. However, because the cosmos is not Krishna's true form, I have not included the Virat Rupa in the list of incarnations."[24]

(3:31) "Revered Suta, this is confusing. If the universe is not the Lord, then how can such meditation have any value?"

The other sages in the assembly nodded their heads in appreciation of the question.

After a moment's thought, Suta replied, "Consider this example. Although both the air and sky are invisible, we refer to the air as dusty or the sky as cloudy. The dust and clouds help us to perceive the existence of the air and sky. Similarly, by seeing the planetary systems as Krishna's personal form, the spiritual novice begins to appreciate that the Lord is a person. However, the actual all-pervasive spiritual form of the Lord is invisible. It is also eternal and indestructible, unlike the planetary systems."

(3:32) Knowing that some yogis meditate on a subtle form of the universe which is unseen, unheard and unmanifest, Shaunaka mentioned this and asked, "Is this a spiritual form of God?"

Suta replied, "No, this is also material."

Shaunaka looked thoughtful. "Since it can be neither seen nor heard then is it also imaginary?"

"No. The subtle form exists. It is the cause of the gross, physical form."

"How can this form be understood?"

"It is like the subtle body of the living being, which carries him from one physical body to another. Just as the living being has his gross and subtle bodies, so does the universe. And as the living being is the soul within the body, so the Lord is the soul of the universe, beyond both its gross and subtle forms."

(3:33) "Since both these meditations are material, please explain how one can conceive of spirit?"

"By the proper culture of transcendental knowledge, one gradually becomes indifferent to the needs of both the subtle and gross material bodies. Only then are we eligible to see both our own eternal spiritual nature as well as the Lord's."

(3:34) Shaunaka looked troubled. "How is it possible to become detached from the demands of the mind and senses? Especially in Kali Yuga; people will find it very difficult."

"This is only possible by Krishna's grace," replied Suta. "When he sees the soul sincerely trying to reach him and praying for release from ignorance, the Lord lifts the curtain of illusion and reveals himself in his all-pervasive, spiritual nature. From this position of Brahman realisation, the repentant soul begins pure devotional service, shining in his own spiritual glory.

(3:35) "So are you saying that we should stop meditating on the gross and subtle forms of the material universe?" asked Shaunaka.

Suta nodded. "Those who are wise reject both these forms and instead worship the unborn Lord, who has no material form or activities and who resides in the heart as the Supersoul. This is the highest knowledge given in the Vedas."

Shaunaka looked around the assembled sages. It seemed from their calm expressions that they accepted Suta's instruction. Perhaps he should address doubts about the difference between the living beings and the Supreme Soul. These were surely widespread.

(3:36) Shaunaka asked, "If the soul is constitutionally spiritual like the Lord, how is it that unlike him our birth and activities are material?"

"Krishna is the abode of all wealth, power, beauty, fame, wisdom and detachment," replied Suta. "He is therefore not influenced by lust, greed, envy or any other material quality. His only reason for coming to the material world is to benefit the fallen souls, whom he accompanies within their hearts. He creates, maintains and destroys the cosmos without being at all affected by material consciousness."

(3:37) Shaunaka drew his brows together. It certainly seemed that Krishna was bewildered by sense objects like an ordinary man. He said, "How can we accept that Krishna is not affected by lust? Did he not have many girlfriends whilst a youth, and later marry thousands of beautiful queens?"

"Krishna cannot be known by observation or mental speculation," said Suta. "No one can understand the Lord's pastimes, names and forms with the material mind, nor explain them by their words since Krishna is beyond the purview of both."

(3:38) "Then how can the Lord be known?"

"Only by rendering unreserved, uninterrupted, favourable service to Krishna, can one know him in his glory, power and transcendence."

(3:39) Shaunaka's head fell. The only way to render such continuous service to Krishna was out of pure love. He said, "How lamentable is my situation, for I have no love for Krishna! How can I ever know him?"

The other sages present voiced agreement. "How can we ever attain such love," said one.

(3:40-42) Suta said, "O learned ones, you are all most fortunate. Inquiring about Krishna and trying to understand the answers is the means of invoking our love for God. Krishna, the proprietor of the universe, guarantees immunity from the dreadful repetition of birth and death to those who seriously make such enquiries."

Many in the audience cheered and Shaunaka said, "Please tell us what we need to hear and understand."

Suta replied, "I shall recite to you the beautiful *Srimad Bhagavatam*, the literary incarnation of God, containing histories of great devotees in direct contact with the Lord. Vyasadeva extracted the cream of the Vedas to compile this unique literature for the benefit of all. Then he taught it to his own son, Shukadeva. He in turn delivered these teachings to King Parikit as he sat surrounded by sages on the bank of the Ganges, where he had retired to fast until death."

(3:43) Recalling the sixth of the sages' original questions, Suta said, "*Srimad Bhagavatam* is brilliant like the sun. It appeared just after Krishna returned to his own abode accompanied by religion and knowledge. People in Kali Yuga, who are suffering due to ignorance, can get guidance from this great literature."

(3:44) Suta bowed his head. "As you know, I had the extraordinary opportunity to hear Shukadeva instruct King Parikit. Since I listened to that conversation with rapt attention, Shukadeva bestowed his mercy on me. Thus I was able to understand the *Bhagavatam*. I shall try to help you comprehend it in the same way, exactly as I understood it from him."

4. Vyasadeva's Confusion

Suta narrates the events preceding Vyasadeva writing the Srimad Bhagavatam. *In trance, Vyasadeva sees a vision of the calamities that will occur in Kali Yuga. Intent on helping the people of that age, he compiles the Vedas and Mahabharata, but still feels dissatisfied. At that time, his spiritual master Narada arrives.*

(4:1-3) A murmur of excitement ran through the audience. The sages were eager to learn more about the *Srimad Bhagavatam*. As they settled down, Shaunaka asked, "O Suta, please tell us in which *yuga*, in what place, and for what reason Sage Vyasadeva undertook this great work. What inspired him to write the *Srimad Bhagavatam*?"

(4:14) Suta replied, "As I am sure you know, Vyasadeva was born as the son of Parasara Muni and Satyavati at the end of Dwapara Yuga. Immediately after his birth, he grew to maturity and left for the Himalayas to practise austerity."

Suta began to relate the story.

***

(4:15-25) Toward the end of the night, Vyasadeva, clad in only a loin cloth, walked by the moonlight to the River Sarasvati. He waded up to his waist into the cool waters. Blocking his nose, ears and eyes with his fingers, he plunged in and out of the water three times. The air was still. There was nobody else in sight. Birds could be heard chirping as the rising sun tinged the eastern horizon with its orange rays. Vyasadeva stood in the river, chanting the Gayatri mantra. A few deer approached the bank and lapped at the water, but Vyasadeva paid no heed. Finishing the Gayatri he began to pray.

"My Lord, how may I serve you? No one should live simply for his own gratification. Please guide me how I can best please you."

For many hours he beseeched the Lord, entering a deep trance of meditation. In his mind's eye he saw prophetic visions of Kali Yuga's coming degradation. The afflicted people would age quickly and die young of disease or violence. Driven by greed, lust and anger, they would destroy the earth, and engage in the mass slaughter of animals and each other.

Horrified by these revelations, Vyasadeva opened his eyes with a start. His heart pounded and sweat ran down his brow. He had to find a way to save the people from their ignorance. For some days he contemplated what to do. Although the Vedas guided people how to piously fulfil their material desires and attain salvation at the end of life, he knew this would be ineffective in the Age of Kali. The scriptures were vast, complicated and not even written down. One had to hear and memorise them. That would be impossible in this age when men's memories would be so poor they would forget what they did the previous day.

Vyasadeva sighed. Bereft of Vedic knowledge, it was no wonder people in Kali Yuga would act abominably, suffering in this life and going to hell after death.

The sage decided to both document the Vedas and organize them into four divisions, named Rig, Yajur, Sama and Atharva. After this, he added a fifth section called the Puranas, historical narrations illustrating the truths taught in the other four Vedas. He laboured for some years, compiling, organising, writing and storing the entire Vedic canon.

Still, he was dissatisfied. Even though they were now recorded, it would still be difficult for any common man to understand them. He therefore entrusted each section to one of his senior disciples to teach. Paila Rishi was given the Rig Veda, Jaimini, the Sama Veda. Vaishampayana, the Yajur Veda, Angira Muni, the Atharva Veda, and Romaharshana, the Puranas.

After training these five students in their respective works, he commanded them, "Go among the people and show them how to understand and apply these teachings. Train your students to teach others, just as I have trained you. Through such spiritual and moral education, hopefully we can save those who will take our help from the ravages of Kali Yuga."

(4:26-31) After his five disciples had departed, Vyasadeva retired to his ashram. He sat in silence, chanting the Lord's names in his mind. For some reason his heart was not peaceful. Although he had now fully presented the Vedas to enable people to achieve life's ultimate goal, he still felt dissatisfied. Only the most intelligent persons would understand even his simplified versions of the Vedas. How could he help ordinary people see the path of true happiness? For some days, he agonised over this problem until at last he became inspired to write the *Mahabharata*, a drama filled with intrigue and romance. This would attract the minds of those unable to study the Vedas. He would weave salient moral truths into the work which would enable people to become happy in this life and attain salvation at the end.

Day and night Vyasadeva wrote, barely eating or sleeping. Despite his tireless efforts, when the *Mahabharata* was finished, he still felt anxious. Confused, he sat in thought for many days. If he was not satisfied after composing these works, how would anyone achieve satisfaction by reading them? What was his mistake? Maybe it was because he had only taught how to become materially happy and attain liberation. He had not explained how to achieve true spiritual satisfaction. This was only possible when one renders loving service to Krishna.

(4:32-33) As Vyasadeva sat outside his cottage on the banks of the Sarasvati, regretting his failings, he heard an angelic voice singing, "Radhika Ramana, Radhika Ramana."

Looking up, he saw the celestial sage, Narada, descending from the airways. Clad in black deerskin and playing his golden lute as he sang, he seemed like a second sun, his golden hair framing his face in a radiant halo.

"Gurudeva!" Vyasadeva called out in exultation. Jumping up, he ran to greet his spiritual master.

After an affectionate exchange, Vyasadeva formally welcomed Narada by washing his feet, garlanding him with forest flowers and offering him refreshment. Then, kneeling before him with folded palms, Vyasadeva said, "Master, I am blessed by your presence."

5. Instructions by Sage Narada

Narada points out the failings in Vyasadeva's plans to alleviate the sufferings he saw in his vision. He encourages Vyasadeva to write the Srimad Bhagavatam. In order to demonstrate the power of these teachings, he relates the history of his past birth in which he first heard Srimad Bhagavatam.

(5:1-4) Smiling, Narada replied, "I divined your discontent, and so I came to you."

Filled with gratitude, Vyasadeva confided in his spiritual master. He told Narada about his visions, and of the efforts he had made to help people in Kali Yuga. He also spoke of his dissatisfaction.

Narada congratulated him on his accomplishments. "You have prepared fine works, including the *Mahabharata*, which is replete with Vedic knowledge. By studying your scholarly compositions, people will learn the best means to attain worldly happiness and liberation. Why then are you unhappy?"

(5:5-7) Sitting before his teacher, Vyasadeva said, "Master, what you say is correct. I have worked hard, but despite this I am not peaceful. Please tell me the root cause of my discontent. As Lord Brahma's son you are a man of unlimited knowledge. You are an exalted devotee of Krishna and can travel anywhere in the universe and beyond. You know the inner heart and feelings of all beings, just like the Supersoul. Please therefore, help me understand my fault, and instruct me how to satisfy the Lord."

(5:8-10) A gentle breeze carried the fragrance of tree blossoms, and peacocks uttered their melodic cries as the two great sages spoke together. Pleased with Vyasadeva's humility, Narada said, "Although you have fully explained the four great aims of life—religious duty, economic development, sense pleasure and liberation—these pertain to the body and mind and cannot satisfy the soul. You have not described Krishna's pure and transcendental glories which alone can make people happy. Any literature bereft of such descriptions is useless."

Vyasadeva bowed his head in acquiescence. This is what he had suspected. Narada had immediately identified the problem.

(5:11) "Write a literature that only glorifies the name, fame, forms, pastimes, qualities, and associates of the unlimited Supreme Lord," said Narada. "Superior to all other Vedas, this will have the potency to transform the impious lives of this world's misdirected civilisation. My dear disciple, glorification of the Lord is so powerful, that even if imperfectly composed, it will still be appreciated by great scholars who are thoroughly honest."

(5:12) Vyasadeva's eyes widened. Normally, if there were grammatical errors in a work, it would be rejected by scholars. What though of ordinary men?

He said, "I doubt that sinful persons will be interested to hear about Krishna. Do they not need to learn piety before they can become amenable to Krishna's service?"

Narada shook his head. "Even if you teach people how to satisfy their material desires religiously, they will still suffer. The only time work in this world does not cause misery is when its fruit is offered for Krishna's pleasure."

Vyasadeva nodded. This was true. No matter how materially prosperous a person becomes, he will not be satisfied. What, though, of liberation?

He asked, "Should I not teach them how to attain salvation before instructing them in devotional topics?"

Narada replied, "If they do not awaken their attraction to Krishna and engage in his loving service, even if they become liberated they will again fall down to material enjoyment."

Vyasadeva raised a hand to his chin. Narada was right. The soul is pleasure seeking. As long as one does not experience the unlimited joy of loving exchanges with Krishna, he will again seek happiness in material pursuits. Vyasadeva accepted that he needed to clearly present Krishna's pastimes. This would be a challenge, as they were deeply esoteric and easily misunderstood.

(5:13) Seeing the anxiety on his disciple's face, Narada encouraged him. "You are a man of impeccable character and firm determination. You are also completely truthful. Therefore, meditate on Krishna and he will reveal to you those pastimes of his which you should describe."

Vyasadeva pressed his lips together. Would materialists have the patience or inclination to read a book exclusively about Krishna's pastimes? He said, "I wrote the *Mahabharata* and other works, so people could hear Krishna's glories, but I first presented material happiness to draw them in. Is this not required for worldly-minded men?"

(5:14-15) Narada waved a hand. "You have committed a serious mistake. This is surely condemned. People are already inclined to sense gratification. By instructing them how to enjoy piously, they will think you are endorsing material enjoyment and will soon neglect the prohibitions. Thus, even while trying to help them, you only render them a great harm. You must write a literature that directly glorifies Krishna. Anything other than this will simply agitate the mind, as the wind tosses a boat on a lake."

"Who in this dark age will read a book that only glorifies God?"

(5:16) Narada said, "In Kali Yuga there will still be discerning people who will appreciate how only devotion to the Supreme Lord can satisfy us. They will benefit from your book, and encourage and help others to follow their example."

(5:17) "Surely even they require training in the social and moral principles governing material life," said Vyasadeva. "Otherwise, they are likely to commit sins which will impede their advancement in devotional service to Krishna."

"Not so," replied Narada "If a person worships Krishna, he may sometimes inadvertently act in a socially or morally inappropriate manner, but there is no danger for him. By Krishna's grace, he will rectify himself and attain spiritual success. On the other hand, even if one meticulously performs all social and moral duties, without worshipping the Lord, he gains no lasting benefit."

"People have material needs whilst in this world," said Vyasadeva. "They have desires for family, society, friendship and love. Do they not need to be shown how to properly satisfy these desires as well?"

(5:18) "Intelligent and thoughtful persons know that even if they achieve heavenly pleasures they will not be happy. Thus, they strive only for divine love, knowing this alone can satisfy the heart."

Seeing Vyasadeva still uncertain, Narada said, "Just as material misery comes unsought, so does material happiness. It cannot be changed. We only enjoy or suffer in this life according to the destiny we have created in previous lives. Therefore, better to use this life to attain eternal and lasting happiness in Krishna's association."

"That is another of my concerns," said Vyasadeva. "What if they do not succeed in returning to Krishna in one life, but instead have to take another birth? Should I not, therefore, teach them how to accumulate piety so that in their next life they are well situated?"

(5:19) "My dear Vyasadeva, even though Krishna's devotee sometimes takes birth again, he does not undergo material existence like others. By Krishna's grace, he will return to devotional service, eager to again experience its sweet taste, which he can never forget."

Vyasadeva folded his palms together and said, "Thank you, Master. I have no more qualms. I will do as you instruct. Please tell me what I should include in this work."

(5:20-21) Narada said, "As well as the process of *bhakti*, you should describe Krishna's unlimited glories. Help your readers understand that Krishna is himself the creation, while remaining aloof from it in his original personal form. Describe the Guna-

Avatars—Brahma, Vishnu and Shiva—through whom he creates, maintains and destroys everything."

He laughed. "You know all this, for you are the Lord's empowered incarnation. You are thus qualified to present his pastimes for the good of all. Please, therefore, describe vividly Krishna's divine activities in the form of *Srimad Bhagavatam.*"

Vyasadeva's face brightened. This was what he had so far omitted. What was the value in teaching people how to fulfil their material desires? He must simply focus on describing Krishna's glories and encourage everyone to take up his devotional service for their ultimate good.

(5:22) Narada continued. "Whatever one hopes to achieve by executing any other work will be accomplished by worshipping Krishna. Indeed, all one's worldly activities should be engaged to spread Krishna's glories. Thus they will become devotional service and will be fully successful."

Master and disciple sat quietly for a moment. Vyasadeva looked across the gleaming waters of the Sarasvati. He would need to first petition the Lord's grace to guide his intelligence. As he sat in thought he heard Narada chuckle and looked at him curiously.

"I was recalling my previous life," Narada said. "I had an unfortunate birth, but because I heard the *Bhagavatam* from four liberated saints, I achieved spiritual perfection. This is why I am urging you to write these same teachings to benefit unfortunate souls."

Vyasadeva humbly asked his spiritual master to relate the history of his past birth.

"In a previous day of Lord Brahma," said Narada, "I was the son of a maidservant. Listen as I recount my story."

***

(5:23-39) "Mother," the small child called plaintively, "I am hungry."

His thin, poorly dressed mother looked at him with tears pricking her eyes. How unfortunate he was to have been born to a maidservant. Her master was a brahmin to whose school many respectable families sent their children. These children were always well-fed and clothed, and spent their time in study or leisure. Her poor child was obliged to work all day. Looking tenderly at her scrawny boy, her tears ran down her cheeks.

"Are you hurt, mother? Shall I help you?"

She laughed at his innocence. "I am also hungry, child. Let us quickly finish cleaning and then we can eat together."

She gave her son a hand broom and began herself polishing brassware. When the chores were done she took the food which had been left and prepared two plates.

"Come, child," she said, taking her son's small hand. "Let us eat."

They had barely finished their meal when her master arrived. She stood up quickly as the kindly looking brahmin entered the room.

"Sit down. Sit down," he said. "Finish your meal."

"Thank you sir, but I have finished now. How may I serve you?"

"Four travelling ascetics have arrived," he announced. "I have invited them to stay here during the rainy season. Would you like to serve them this year?" He always gave the servants a chance to attend holy men who arrived. In this and other ways, he tried to help them attain a better destiny in their future lives.

The woman folded her palms and thanked him. "I would be honoured for such an opportunity."

"Very well, but remember they are monks," he said. "They do not like to be too close to women. You can get your son to directly serve their meals, while you cook and clean."

For the next four months, the child waited upon the four elderly brahmin*s*. After serving their food, he would sit nearby waiting on them as they ate and would thereby hear their conversations. The ascetics took a liking to the boy.

"He is very sober for such a young child," one remarked.

Another asked him, "What do you like to play, boy?"

"I don't play, sir," replied the child. "I help my mother with her work." After a pause he added, "I do enjoy listening to your stories."

The men all laughed. "Well, boy," said one of them, "if you like, you can sit with us whenever we talk. Then you can hear more of our stories."

"I would like that very much, sir."

"You must not interrupt or make a noise," warned the ascetic.

"No sir, I promise to be good."

From that day, if the boy was ever absent when the saints were talking, they would ask his master, "Where is the lad? Please send him here."

Seeing the attachment the holy men had for the child, the master told his mother to excuse him from any other chores.

"He should remain with them as much as possible. They seem to like him," he said, patting the boy's head.

On one occasion, as the ascetics spoke, one of them mentioned that to eat the remnants of saints brings about great good fortune. Hearing this, the boy wondered if he could receive any of their food. He would have to ask them for a portion, as they only ate small amounts and never left anything on their plates.

That afternoon, after serving their meal, he got up his courage and meekly said, "This morning you explained that it brings great fortune to eat the food left by saintly persons."

"Yes," replied the ascetics, surprised that he had been listening so attentively.

Blushing, the boy asked, "May I eat some of your remnants?"

The four saints' hearts melted on seeing the child's simple faith. "Yes, boy," they replied. "We will give you some, but we can only do it once, as, really, it is against our regulative principles."

The boy held out his right hand and they each placed a morsel of food in it. As he placed their remnants in his mouth, he felt a deep peace pervade his heart. His eagerness to learn from the saints intensified. He continued to listen attentively to all their discourses. Because they told him it is good to repeat what he had heard, in the evenings he would explain everything to his tired and sleepy mother.

Gradually, his taste for hearing increased until his mind was absorbed in their teachings. They trained him in their other spiritual practices, such as chanting Krishna's holy names, and worshipping his form. He slowly became free of material contamination, and in due course realised that he was not actually a poor boy. He was a spiritual being, a fragmental part of the Lord, qualitatively the same as him. During the four months they stayed at the brahmin's school, the saints instructed him in all the

41

confidential truths of bhakti yoga, known as the *Srimad Bhagavatam*.

"How will I continue with my devotional service when you have left?" the boy enquired. "I will be obliged to again serve and associate with materialistic men, and I may fall from the path of pure devotion."

The ascetics instructed him to do his duties as an offering for Krishna's pleasure. "In that consciousness, your work will become devotional service to the Lord, and you will never again fall into ignorance or be entangled by the reactions of work."

"O holy ones, how can I offer my work to the Lord?"

"Whilst doing your chores, which you should see as your God-given duty, simultaneously remember Krishna by meditating either on his name, activities, instructions, or qualities. In this way, the same work which binds one to material existence becomes the cause of liberation, and your transcendental knowledge will increase."

Initiating him into a sacred mantra, the ascetics taught the boy how he could mentally worship the Lord's form. "Dear child, always meditate on this mantra: I offer respect to Lord Krishna along with his plenary expansions Vasudeva, Pradyumna, Aniruddha, and Sankarshana."

The boy diligently followed their instructions, confident that he would soon achieve spiritual perfection.

6. Narada's Previous Life

Narada further describes his past birth, which culminates in his seeing Lord Vishnu and receiving his eternal spiritual form.

(6:1-19) When the rainy season ended, the saintly brahmins departed. The boy continued assisting his mother, while always remembering Krishna, as they had instructed him. He would rise early and worship the Lord in his mind, chanting the mantra they had taught him. Seeing his devotional inclinations, his mother did her best to give him time for his spiritual practices. She would work harder than all the other servants, so that her son need not do as much. Still, whenever her master would see the boy not working, he would give him jobs. So despite her best efforts, the woman was unable to do anything to help her son. Even so, the boy was not disturbed because he knew everything happened by Krishna's divine arrangement.

One night, the master wanted milk. "Send the lad to the cowsheds," he told the boy's mother. Not wanting to disturb her son who was absorbed in meditation, she took the vessel and went out into the dark. As she walked by the scant moonlight she stepped on a coiled snake which immediately bit her. She screamed in pain and terror, and stumbled back to her room. There she collapsed to the floor and writhed in agony in front of her alarmed son. "Snake!" she cried repeatedly.

The boy ran over and knelt by his mother, frantically examining her to find the bite. The venom quickly coursed through her veins. Within a few minutes, the woman died as her son loudly chanted Krishna's name.

The boy cradled his mother and wept, stroking her forehead. Why had Krishna let this happen? Was it to make him detached? As long as his mother lived, he would have stayed to assist her. The Lord, however, had taken her. He now had no reason to stay there in the association of materialists. Out of his causeless mercy, Krishna had freed him from all obligation. Surely he should leave at once. Unseen by anyone, the boy immediately walked out into the night, taking only a blanket wrapped around his shoulders. Following the light of the pole star which the ascetics had once shown him, he headed toward the north, determined to become an ascetic.

So that the master would not find him, he left the main path and walked through the dense jungle. That night, he curled up beneath a tree with his blanket around him and slept. By Krishna's arrangement he was not troubled by wild animals, and the next day he continued his journey. Day after day, month after month, and year after year, the boy walked, surviving on fruits and wild roots, continuously chanting his mantra. Gradually, hunger and thirst no longer troubled him as he became fixed in spiritual consciousness. Occasionally when he passed through a city or town, some kind person would offer him a cooked meal. The boy grew into a man. Still, he continued to roam about, just as his spiritual masters had done before him. He walked through flourishing cities, towns, villages, farms, mines, agricultural lands, valleys, flower gardens and forests. When people saw the young bearded mendicant, they would come to hear spiritual discourses from him, and he would repeat for their benefit all he had heard from his own teachers.

As he grew older, he desired more solitude to practise meditation and headed for the wilderness. He passed through mountains coloured by great veins of gold and silver, and large freshwater lakes with lotus flowers, beautified by bees and singing birds. Admiring the celestial beauty of his surroundings, he felt he was in heaven.

At other times, he entered dark fearsome forests, dense with reeds and thorny bushes, and inhabited by snakes, owls, and baying jackals. When he felt exhausted, he would bathe in clear mountain lakes and drink their cool water. Feeling refreshed, he would sit under the shade of a tree and meditate on Krishna with feelings of ecstatic love, intoning his mantra, his eyes brimming with tears of longing to see the Lord.

On one such occasion, as he sat under a banyan tree in an uninhabited forest meditating on Krishna, the Lord appeared within his heart. His body erupted with goose pimples and his mind was overcome with ecstasy. Suddenly, Krishna's form disappeared. No longer seeing his beloved Lord, he cried out in the grief of separation. He jumped up and frantically looked about, like a person who has lost a great treasure.

"Krishna! Krishna! Where have you gone?" He repeatedly called as he searched the forest groves.

When he could not find Krishna anywhere, he sat down again in meditation, desperate for another vision of his Lord. Not seeing Krishna even in his heart, he breathed heavily. Hot tears streamed down his cheeks, he felt dizzy and kept calling out, "Krishna! Krishna! Where are you? Why have you left me? O my Lord! My Lord!"

(6:20-26) Suddenly, he heard an ethereal voice address him affectionately. "My dear devotee, I have revealed myself to you because of your sincere and determined practice. Never do I show myself to those careless in their worship. I appeared before you in order to increase your yearning for my eternal association. Such intense hankering for me destroys all material desires. As that longing intensifies, my devotee's pure love for me gradually deepens."

The Lord told him the reason for his great good fortune was the training he had received from the four ascetics. He assured him that if he continued to follow their instructions, he would become the Lord's associate in the transcendental world after leaving his body.

A fear arose in his heart. What if he should forget the Lord at the time of death? Understanding his anxiety, the Lord reassured him. "Whatever advancement you make will never be destroyed. Your transcendental knowledge and love for me will stay with you birth after birth, until it fully matures. Then you will return to me."

Feeling grateful, the young ascetic bowed his head in obeisance. He then resumed his travels, chanting the Lord's glories without inhibition wherever he went. His mind was completely satisfied; he envied no one and had no pride.

He spent the remainder of his life absorbed in thoughts of Krishna. Wherever he travelled, he spread the Lord's glories. He was free of all material attachments and aversions. When the allotted time of his death arrived, he instantaneously received an eternal, indestructible, spiritual body befitting an associate of the Lord.

***

Vyasadeva sat mesmerized as Narada finished his tale.

(6:27-28) "As a young boy I had no spiritual discernment, but I associated with those four great *sannyasis*, who possessed pure devotion and profound knowledge of the Absolute Truth. I heard from them the *Srimad Bhagavatam* and achieved a most wonderful result."

(6:40) Looking pointedly at Vyasadeva, Narada said, "Therefore, I ask that you simply describe Krishna's pastimes. By so doing, you will fully satisfy the pious, and then they will be able to uplift others by their association."

(6:29-32) Vyasadeva nodded slowly. Narada's personal testimony was powerful. Still he had a doubt. "Master, since you attained your eternal spiritual body at that time, how is it you have now taken birth as Brahma's son?"

Narada said, "Just as the eternally spiritual Lord descends into the world to reclaim the fallen souls, similarly I also appeared. When Narayana lay down in the causal waters of creation, I entered with his breath, and then was born from Brahma's deliberation."

Narada explained how the difference between himself and Brahma's other sons was that his body is spiritual, but the other sages took birth in material bodies.

"Since I appeared in my own spiritual body, I am free to travel anywhere within the material creation, and also to the spiritual worlds without impediment. Wherever I go, I play my transcendental lute and sing the Lord's glories for the benefit of all souls."

(6:33-36) Vyasadeva said, "After attaining his association, are you not now feeling unhappiness being separated from the Lord?"

Narada laughed. "I am never apart from my Lord. As soon as I glorify him, he appears in my heart, as if summoned."

Vyasadeva looked at his spiritual master in awe. Narada again became grave. "My dear Vyasadeva, I have told you my history in order to persuade you to exclusively describe the Lord's glories. The conditioned souls suffering in this material world will not attain satisfaction even by gratifying their senses piously, nor indeed by renouncing sense gratification. Constant hearing and chanting about Krishna is the only suitable boat for helping all souls cross the ocean of material suffering and dissatisfaction."

***

(6:37-38) Suta said, "Narada then took leave of Vyasadeva, and whilst playing his lute, he ascended into the sky and disappeared."

Folding his palms, Suta praised Narada. "All glory and success to the illustrious Narada, because in great joy, he always extols the Lord, travelling throughout the universe to save the suffering souls."

Shaunaka and the sages lifted their arms into the air and enthusiastically exclaimed, "All praise to Narada!"

7. The Pandavas and Krishna

In answer to Shaunaka's queries, Suta relates three stories: Vyasadeva's meditation after Narada's departure; Shukadeva's history; and the background of Parikit's birth. In so doing he gives a dramatic account of the events following the Pandavas' victory at Kurukshetra.

(7:1-3) When calm again prevailed, Shaunaka asked, "What did Vyasadeva do after Narada left?"

Suta replied that Vyasadeva remained at his hermitage on the western bank of the River Sarasvati. "In a small cottage surrounded by berry trees he sat down and began to meditate."

"Why did the great sage not leave home to engage in spiritual practice, as is the custom?"

"Vyasadeva's ashram is situated at Samyaprasha where he had previously compiled the Vedas," replied Suta. "He stayed there because the atmosphere is most suitable for spiritual engagement. Please listen as I tell you what transpired."

***

(7:4-7) Meditating with a completely tranquil mind, Vyasadeva, in trance, saw Krishna. With him were his energies and expansions, including the living entities. Behind the Lord stood Maya, the material energy.

Vyasadeva saw the souls being allured by Maya. By her influence, they falsely identified with matter and began to suffer material existence. He became pensive. Plainly, the soul's perverted attraction for Maya was the cause of their delusion and suffering. How could they be saved? Then he saw some souls developing an attraction for Krishna. As their love for Krishna increased, the Lord ordered Maya to release them, and they awoke to their blissful spiritual identity. Vyasadeva was astonished. How had this happened?

As he continued to meditate, he realised they were hearing narrations of Krishna's pastimes and glories. The *Srimad Bhagavatam*! He saw how by listening to the sacred text, the materially conditioned souls' love for Krishna blossomed. They became enthusiastic to exclusively serve him; thus attracting his protection. Of course! That was Narada's point. Simply by hearing *Srimad Bhagavatam,* an attraction for the Lord's loving service sprouts up in the heart, extinguishing the fire of lamentation, illusion and fearfulness.

Vyasadeva fell to the ground, overwhelmed with ecstasy. The Lord was so great and merciful that one only had to hear about him to become free of ignorance and pain. He shed profuse tears of joy. Gradually he calmed himself, and immediately began to write the *Srimad Bhagavatam*.

***

(7:8-11) Suta concluded his description, "When the divine literature was completed, Vyasadeva taught it to his son, Shukadeva."

"How was that possible?" Shaunaka asked. "I have heard that Shukadeva, who was self-realised from birth, left home before even receiving the customary rites of passage."

Suta replied, "You have heard correctly, my dear friend. Shukadeva went to a solitary place to meditate on the impersonal Brahman. However, when Vyasadeva completed his work, he instructed two of his disciples to go to his son and recite several verses of the *Srimad Bhagavatam*. Upon hearing these verses, Shukadeva's heart became attracted to Krishna, and he returned to his father's ashram to receive further instructions from him."[25]

Shaunaka remained doubtful. "What need is there for a fully self-realised soul, who is already detached from family connections, to learn the *Srimad Bhagavatam*?"

A broad smile lit up Suta's face. "My dear friends," he said, "not only can the beautiful narrations of Krishna's pastimes liberate suffering souls, but they also appeal to liberated souls. Although such elevated personalities have no interest in fleeting sensual pleasure, they take great delight in hearing these transcendental discourses. Thus, even though Shukadeva was immersed in Brahman meditation, when he overheard the devotees reciting the *Bhagavatam,* his heart was profoundly attracted to Krishna, and he desired to hear more."

"Pray tell us the verses which enchanted Shukadeva's mind."

Suta replied, "The first, spoken to Yudhisthira by Bhishma, was, 'O king, that person whom, out of

51

ignorance only, you thought to be your maternal cousin, your very dear friend, well-wisher, counsellor, messenger and benefactor, is the Personality of Godhead, Krishna.

"The next verse was spoken by the great devotee, Uddhava. 'Alas, how shall I take shelter of one more merciful than he who granted the position of mother to the she-demon, Putana, although she was faithless, and smeared her breast with deadly poison for the Lord to suck?"

Suta recited another verse, and when he had finished, many of the sages sat stunned in ecstasy, others wept, and still others laughed ecstatically.[26]

Shaunaka's limbs trembled and his bodily hairs stood erect. Gradually, he composed himself and said, "My mind is bewildered. I had other questions, but I can hardly remember them. All I want now is to hear more about Krishna."

Suta, who was also feeling overwhelmed with spiritual emotion, encouraged his friend. "Let us not leave any room for doubts. Take a moment to remember your questions."

Shaunaka straightened himself and breathed deeply. Gradually, his memory returned. "You told us that Shukadeva recited the *Srimad Bhagavatam* to Parikit, when the emperor was fasting to death by the banks of the Ganges."

"Yes," replied Suta. "What is the confusion?"

(4:6-14) Shaunaka answered, "I have heard that Shukadeva walked about naked, pretending to be dumb and senseless so that materialistic people would not speak to him. Indeed, I have also heard that he was generally considered to be mad."

Laughing, he related an incident he had heard demonstrating Shukadeva's aloofness from material existence. "Once, Shukadeva, naked as usual, wandered near a lake where a group of celestial damsels were bathing. These ladies had not been disturbed to see him, as he made no distinction between male and female. When Vyasadeva, following his son, passed by them, those same ladies quickly covered themselves. This was because, unlike Shukadeva, it was apparent Vyasadeva recognised the difference between male and female. Unfortunately, most people interpret Shukadeva's detachment to be the sign of insanity, so how did Parikit recognise him to be a self-realised soul and agree to hear from him?"

Suta said, "Ah, wonderful question. I will explain. Do you have any other doubts?"

Shaunaka replied, "It also amazes me that Shukadeva agreed to instruct Emperor Parikit for seven days and nights. I have been told that normally, he never associated with materialists for longer than it took to receive a cup of milk. Even that brief connection was simply in order to benefit the giver. Actually, he did not need their charity as he depended fully on Krishna. So how is it that he sat for one week with the world emperor?"

Suta said, "Another excellent question! Do you have any further queries?"

Shaunaka continued. "I am also intrigued as to why Emperor Parikit gave up his kingdom to fast to death. So many citizens depended on his leadership and protection. As a great devotee, surely he had a sense of responsibility for everyone's welfare. Even other kings looked to him for guidance and protection. He was not materially attached and performed his kingly duties in the spirit of pure devotional service to Krishna. So why did he give up his God-given duty and fast to death?"

(7:12-13) Shaunaka stopped and sat back. He shook his head slightly. "Am I wasting our time with these questions? Maybe you should just tell us about Krishna. After hearing those sublime verses, I think we only want to hear his glories."

Some sages in the assembly called out in agreement. "Yes, please tell us about Krishna's pastimes."

Others, however, disagreed. "We also had these doubts that Shaunaka expressed. Please first dispel them for us."

Suta held up his hands to quieten the audience. "My friends, be peaceful. I shall speak about Krishna's pastimes while simultaneously answering your questions. You need, first, to understand about Parikit's exalted birth and heritage. He was the posthumous son of Abhimanyu, the son of Arjuna and Subhadra. Thus, the emperor was Krishna's grand-nephew."

Shaunaka expressed surprise. "Parikit was directly related to Krishna?"

Suta nodded. "Certainly."

Shaunaka's face lit up. "I think I understand how he was able to recognize Shukadeva, and why that esteemed sage spent so much time with him. As Krishna's relation, Parikit must have been a great saint himself."

"Yes, you have understood my point. He was a pure devotee from his very birth. Indeed, he saw the Lord in the womb when the Kaurava warrior, Ashvatthama, tried to kill him with the Brahmastra missile."

Shaunaka frowned. "Why did Ashvatthama hurl that most deadly weapon at an unborn child? And how is it Parikit did not die at that time?"

"I will explain," replied Suta. "Let us pick up the story from the first day after the Pandavas defeated Duryodhana in the Battle of Kurukshetra."

(7:14-57) Yudhisthira sat amid his brothers, along with Draupadi and Krishna. They had just spent their victory night in Duryodhana's deserted tent. Finally, the nightmare of their persecution at the Kurus' hands was over.

"You have a long day ahead of you, Emperor," said Krishna. "After breakfast, you should return to your own camp and meet with your generals."

As they broke their fast, a commotion arose outside. They heard the shrill voice of a hysterical man demanding to see the Emperor, and the gruff tones of guards forbidding him, followed by the sounds of a scuffle. Concerned, Yudhisthira asked for the distressed man to be brought before him.

Soon a disheveled and shaking man entered, flanked by two armed guards. Seeing Yudhisthira, he fell flat to the ground weeping. "My lord," he cried, "they are all dead!"

"Who?" asked Yudhisthira, "and who are you, my good sir?"

The man remained weeping on the floor, repeatedly muttering, "They are all dead!"

Intrigued, Bhima rose from his seat and helped the trembling newcomer to his feet. Examining him closely, he exclaimed, "Aapt!"

The man touched Bhima's feet in respect. "Yes lord, it is I."

Bhima turned to Yudhisthira and said, "He is a cook in your army, brother."

Greeted warmly by the Pandavas and Krishna, Aapt was encouraged to speak. He told them how the previous night the head cook had ordered him to go to the river to collect water for breakfast. When he returned, he saw the camp ablaze, and he could hear men screaming. He hurried toward the entrance where he saw Kripacharya in full armour holding a drawn sword and guarding the gate. As he approached him, some panicked soldiers rushed out of the camp. To Aapt's horror, Kripacharya mercilessly cut down those unarmed and frightened men. Terrified, Aapt then hid in the bushes.

Around an hour later, Ashvatthama emerged, covered in blood, holding his sword aloft in one hand, and in the other, a large sack from which blood dripped endlessly. Laughing like a madman, he asked Kripacharya, "Did any escape?"

"A few tried, but I killed them just as you ordered, General."

Aapt continued, "When the two had left I entered our camp. Going from tent to tent, I saw that everyone had been slain."

"My sons? My brothers?" cried Draupadi, jumping up from her seat in extreme agitation.

Aapt looked down and made no reply. As the Pandavas stared at him in horror, Draupadi swooned.

Meanwhile on the battlefield, Duryodhana lay with his leg awkwardly trapped under his thigh, his drawn sword on the bare earth by his side. As the sun brightened the horizon, the snarling jackals surrounding him backed off. Exhausted from his efforts to keep them at bay, he tried to lie back but could not because of his leg's awkward position. Gently, he attempted to ease his limb down, but unbearable pain seared through his body and made him cry out in anguish. Strenuously keeping himself propped up with his elbows, he looked down at his bloodied thigh. He cursed Bhima. How could that evil-minded Pandava have struck him below the waist? Duryodhana's breath came rapidly. He did not have the strength to keep himself up for much longer. Gritting his teeth, he made one more herculean effort to dislodge his foot and straighten his leg. The pain was so severe he lost consciousness.

Slowly coming round, he heard a low voice say, "Curses on those loathsome Pandavas. Look what they have done to the king."

A heavy hand stroked Duryodhana's brow, and he felt cool water on his lips. Slowly opening his eyes, he saw a blur which gradually formed into Ashvatthama's face.

"Thank God you still live!" Ashvatthama cried out.

Duryodhana closed his eyes. Hot tears streamed down his face. "My friend," he rasped. "All is lost. I cannot survive much longer. Flee while you can."

Ashvatthama spoke heatedly, "My lord, I have wreaked revenge on your enemies. I single-handedly killed the Pandavas and their entire army."

Duryodhana again opened his eyes with difficulty, straining against the pain that racked his whole body.

"The Pandavas are dead?" he exclaimed. He looked doubtfully at his general. How could Ashvatthama alone have accomplished what he with all his royal resources had not been able to achieve throughout his entire life?

"I cannot believe you," he cried.

"I have proof!" Ashvatthama declared. "See what I have brought!"

Ashvatthama picked up the bloodied sack which lay on the ground next to him and tipped out its macabre contents. Five severed heads rolled onto the ground, their sightless eyes staring out of their pallid faces.

"I killed them while they slept," said Ashvatthama, with a harsh laugh.

Duryodhana strained to recognize the five faces of his enemies. "Let me touch them, I will be able to tell their features with my hands."

Ashvatthama placed the decapitated head of Bhima's son in Duryodhana's hands. "Behold the head of your nemesis Bhima!"

Duryodhana eagerly ran his fingers over the nose, eyes and mouth. Yes, this was Bhima. He was finally slain! Duryodhana thanked Providence he had lived long enough to see the death of his sworn enemy.

"I congratulate you on your chivalry, General Ashvatthama!"

As Ashvatthama smiled proudly, Duryodhana curled his fingers around the skull and squeezed it, imagining he was personally destroying Bhima. To his surprise and dismay, it caved in under a little pressure.

"This cannot be Bhima's skull! His entire body is like iron."

Turning disappointedly toward Ashvatthama, he demanded, "Tell me the truth! Who was this man?"

Ashvatthama sighed. "Very well, it is not Bhima but his son, Sutasoma. These other four are Draupadi's other sons."

"Why did you lie to me?"

"The son is considered the same as the father, so I did not exactly lie," protested Ashvatthama.

"You heinous fool!" exclaimed Duryodhana.

Shrinking back in shame, Ashvatthama said, "I just wanted to make you happy before you left."

Duryodhana's head fell back to the ground in despair, and he snarled, "How could you think this vile act would please me? I had no quarrel with these boys. They were the last surviving males in our dynasty. How will the Kurus survive now?"

Grimacing with pain, Duryodhana turned his head away from Ashvatthama. "Leave me! I do not want to see your face."

Ashvatthama stood up, his face a mask of dismay. Looking around fearfully, he stumbled back toward his horse. If Duryodhana was so disgusted with him, he dared not imagine what the Pandavas were thinking. He needed to flee before they found him.

In Duryodhana's royal tent, the five Pandavas and Krishna gently tried to revive Draupadi. Picking her up in his arms, Bhima placed her on a couch. They wiped her forehead with a damp cloth. When she opened her eyes, she again remembered the frightful news, and cried piteously, "Oh my sons! My sons!"

His grief and fury rising, Arjuna picked up his bow known as the Gandiva and addressed his inconsolable wife. "Gentle lady, when I present you with that wretched brahmin's head, after beheading him with arrows from my Gandiva bow, I shall wipe the tears from your eyes and pacify you. Then, after burning your sons' bodies, you can take your ritual bath standing on his head."

Touching Yudhisthira's feet, he requested, "Grant me permission to depart, dear brother."

Yudhisthira nodded, "Go, but be cautious, Arjuna. Ashvatthama has lost all sense of morality. He is unpredictable and dangerous.

Krishna stepped forward, and also touched Yudhisthira's feet. "Please allow me to accompany my friend."

Yudhisthira smiled and gave his assent. He looked lovingly at Krishna. Who could understand him? The whole world moves under his command, and yet he humbly asks permission from his servant.

The two friends hurried to Arjuna's chariot. Krishna climbed into the driving seat and took the reins. Clutching his bow, Arjuna jumped up behind Krishna. He held on to the chariot's pole as Krishna urged the horses on and they sped away in clouds of dust.

Some distance ahead of them, Ashvatthama repeatedly whipped his fatigued horse, frequently glancing over his shoulder. Seeing the dust in the distance raised by Arjuna's chariot, he became even more frantic. It could only be the vengeful Pandavas pursuing him. They would surely show him no mercy. Like a madman, Ashvatthama strapped his horse relentlessly. Without warning, his animal collapsed in exhaustion, pitching him headlong onto the ground. Scrambling over to an outcrop of rocks, he lay flat behind them, his heart pounding. He peered out and saw a single chariot, flying Arjuna's flag, rapidly approaching. Ashvatthama knew he could not possibly defeat Arjuna in fair combat. His hands shaking with terror, he took his bow from his back. Quickly setting an arrow to the string, he called to mind the mantras to invoke the ultimate weapon known as the Brahmastra.

Krishna, who was driving Arjuna's chariot, noticed Ashvatthama's fallen steed. "Look," he called out to Arjuna, "there is his horse. He must be nearby."

Suddenly the sky was filled with a brilliant glare. Nothing could be seen anywhere. His heart pounding with fear, Arjuna called out to Krishna, "O Krishna, Krishna! Mighty-armed Lord! Only you can bestow fearlessness in your devotees! You alone can deliver everyone burning in the inferno of material existence. Please save me from this fearful fire."

Krishna called back, "What are you saying, Arjuna? I am your cousin. I am just like you. What do you think I can do to save us?"

"My Lord, I know who you are. You are the original controller, beyond the material energy. Your body is not material like mine. It is purely spiritual. You are the original Personality of Godhead. Although you expand yourself as the all-pervading Supersoul, you still remain untouched by the material energy. Though you have full control of material nature, it never contaminates you. You always remain blissful and in full knowledge. All suffering souls can attain freedom from the miseries of material existence by seeking your guidance alone. O transcendental one, you descend to remove the earth's burden and benefit your friends, especially those rapt in your thought. Please therefore tell me, what is this terrible effulgence?"

"Arjuna, you are a mighty warrior. Do you not recognise the glare of the dreadful Brahmastra weapon?"

Arjuna's eyes grew wide. "Did Ashvatthama release it?"

"Yes."

"He does not know how to withdraw the weapon. Drona only taught that to me. Unchecked, it may destroy the world."

"Fear makes a man reckless, Arjuna. You must quickly neutralise this threat. Release your own Brahmastra!"

Arjuna looked shocked. "Two Brahmastras fired at once?! Surely that will annihilate the planet."

Krishna reassured him. "With an unperturbed mind, you must chant the mantras for withdrawal as soon as the two bombs meet, before their radiation causes devastation. Your timing must be precise."

Arjuna touched water for purification. Then, after offering respects to Krishna, he fitted an arrow to his bow and intoned the mantras to invoke the Brahmastra. He released it with a resounding twang from the Gandiva. The blazing arrow streaked upward and as it collided with Ashvatthama's Brahmastra, a great circle of fire appeared in the sky. Everyone felt scorched by its heat but Arjuna instantly withdrew the weapons, and the fire at once subsided.

Seeing that his missile had been neutralised, Ashvatthama got up and sprinted toward the nearby forest. Spotting him, Arjuna jumped down from his chariot and gave chase. He hurled himself at the fleeing Ashvatthama and knocked him to the ground. Arjuna pounded him almost senseless and then dragged him back to his chariot where Krishna stood waiting.

"Why did you not just kill him with your arrows?" Krishna demanded angrily, as Arjuna bound his captive hand and foot. "Why are you showing him any mercy? Kill him immediately, for without any compunction he slew innocent boys in their sleep."

"My Lord, why do you ask me to act sinfully? You know the warrior code better than I. An enemy who is careless, intoxicated, insane, asleep, afraid, or devoid of his chariot should not be slain. For that reason, I have spared his life."

Krishna persisted. "You do not properly understand the codes, Arjuna. If you did, you would know that a cruel and wretched person who lives at the cost of others' lives deserves to be killed for his own benefit. By punishing him with death, you will save him from hell."

"Lord, let him first be judged by Yudhisthira. Let that righteous monarch condemn him to death and thereby save his soul. I cannot kill a man unfairly in combat."

Arjuna bundled Ashvatthama onto the chariot and then climbed aboard.

Krishna was not assuaged. "You promised Draupadi you would bring back his severed head. Why are you breaking your word? How do you think she will feel, seeing her sons' murderer alive and well on your chariot?"

Remembering his aggrieved wife, Arjuna softly replied, "I do not want to add to that blessed lady's misery. She would not like to see me defile myself with sin. Let Ashvatthama be tried by the Emperor. When he decrees it, I will kill him."

Krishna smiled to himself, seeing his friend's determination to judiciously apply religious principles. On the battlefield of Kurukshetra, in a moment of uncharacteristic rashness, Arjuna almost lost his good intelligence and was ready to kill his brother Yudhisthira for the sake of a trivial vow. Krishna had then instructed him about the importance of weighing up which religious principle should take precedence in any situation. Clearly Arjuna had taken those instructions to heart. Controlling his mind, he was refusing to be goaded into acting hastily. Krishna decided to test him a little further. Had he fully conquered his anger, which impels even sober men to act sinfully?

Feigning anger, Krishna challenged Arjuna. "Why are you showing him clemency? Look at him! For no one's gain, he treacherously assassinated all your sons and surviving relatives. Not even his own master, Duryodhana, was pleased with him. Kill him immediately. He is the disgrace of his family."

Arjuna smiled. "My dear friend, I know your nature. Surely you are testing me. Everything you have said regarding why I should kill him is true. On the other hand, it is forbidden to disrespect or harm the family members of one's guru. Since his father was my worshipful martial teacher, I wish to first confer with Yudhisthira, who is religion personified."

Laughing, Krishna warmly embraced Arjuna. "Let us return to camp and see what King Yudhisthira orders."

Hearing the thunderous sound of a chariot approaching, the Pandavas accompanied by Satyaki and Draupadi came out to greet Arjuna. When Krishna drew the chariot to a stop next to them, Draupadi saw Ashvatthama bound like a captured animal sitting silently on the floor of the chariot, his head down.

She was horrified to see him in such a condition. Folding her hands together, her voice filled with compassion, she respectfully greeted her sons' killer. "My obeisance to you, son of Drona."

Turning her face up to Arjuna, she pleaded, "Release him! He is a brahmin, and to be respected like our guru."

Bhima, fearing Arjuna might indeed free him, exclaimed, "He is no brahmin. He killed our sons while they slept! Punish him!"

Draupadi objected. "His father taught you everything you know about military arts. The father lives in the son. Ashvatthama should thus be revered like your teacher. Besides that, the gentle Kripi did not immolate herself at the time of Drona's cremation because she still had a surviving son. If you kill him, it will be as good as killing that devoted lady."

Yudhisthira, Arjuna, Nakula and Sahadeva all nodded in agreement. Seeing them swayed by Draupadi, Bhima protested, "Women are naturally soft-hearted, and this can influence their proper discrimination in judicial matters. This man is a heinous murderer. For his own benefit, he should be executed at once. Otherwise, in his next life, he will suffer in hell for his crime."

Draupadi approached Yudhisthira and pleaded with him, "O virtuous one! You are celebrated for your high character! You should not cause suffering to your guru's family. They should be respected and worshipped."

"He is not worthy to be called Drona's son," argued Bhima. "He is a disgrace to the brahmins! O Emperor, do not let your judgment be influenced by a sentimental woman."

Draupadi turned to Bhima. "Dear husband, do not make Ashvatthama's mother, Kripi, cry as I do, pained by my sons' deaths."

Turning back to Yudhisthira, she argued, "If the kings of this world offend the brahmins, they will be destroyed by the fire of their anger. Therefore, please release this man."

Yudhisthira reassured Draupadi. "Your words are in accord with the principles of religion, my dear wife, and are full of mercy and equity."

He turned to his other brothers, as well as Satyaki and Krishna to gauge their feelings. All of them, except Bhima, agreed that Draupadi had spoken wisely.

Bhima stepped forward. "I can understand a gentle woman thinking like this," he said, looking around at the men. "How, though, can you heroes who know the principles of governance think he should be released?"

Bhima paced slowly from one man to the other. He pointed at Ashvatthama and spat out his words. "This man is a wanton criminal. He murdered sleeping youths for no purpose; neither furthering his own interest nor his master's. He acted out of pure malice and must be punished for his own good."

Yudhisthira looked to Krishna. "My Lord, you are the origin of religion. What is your decision?"

Krishna said, "Draupadi is right when she says even a fallen brahmin should not be slain. However, Bhima also speaks correctly when he says that an aggressor must be killed. These are both scriptural edicts."

Turning to Arjuna, he put a hand on his shoulder. "You must find a way of satisfying all parties, my dear friend."

Arjuna stood in thought. During the battle of Kurukshetra, he was faced with the dilemma of either keeping his promise and killing Yudhisthira, or not harming Yudhisthira but breaking his promise. Krishna had expertly shown him how to both maintain his vow and let Yudhisthira live. Now, the Lord wanted to see him similarly solve this problem. Arjuna raised his great sword in his right hand, and with his other hand he grabbed Ashvatthama's bound hair.

Ashvatthama cried out, "Spare me! Spare me!"

Arjuna swung his sword in a swift arc and lopped off the jewel on Ashvatthama's head along with his knotted hair. Ashvatthama fell to the ground, shaking in shock.

Handing the jewel to Draupadi, Arjuna said, "Because this jewel always adorns Ashvatthama's head, cutting it off is like severing his head. Thus have I kept my promise, while honouring your desire to not harm him."

Turning to his brothers and Krishna, Arjuna explained, "Cutting the hair from his head, taking away his wealth, and banishing him from his residence are the prescribed punishments for a fallen brahmin. There is no injunction for killing his body."

Yudhisthira embraced his brother and praised his good intelligence. Turning to Ashvatthama, who sat slumped on the ground, he said, "Do not stay in Hastinapura. Leave my dominion and never return."

His body filthy with the dried blood of his victims, his unevenly shorn hair giving him a comical appearance, Ashvatthama, bowed his head in humiliation, and slunk off to live as an exile in the wilderness. His mind burned with a desire for revenge.

The Pandavas were satisfied. This insult was as good as death for the proud Ashvatthama.[27]

8. Krishna Saves His Devotees

As Krishna is preparing to depart for Dwaraka, Ashvatthama releases six Brahmastra weapons to destroy the Pandavas and their unborn grandchild. Krishna personally saves them. Overwhelmed with gratitude, Queen Kunti, the Pandavas' mother, offers him prayers. Yudhisthira then convinces Krishna to stay longer in Hastinapura.

(8:1-4) Seated on covered palanquins, the royal ladies, headed by Kunti, Gandhari and Draupadi, led the funeral procession to the Ganges where the deceased's last rites would be performed. With their disheveled hair hanging loose and their eyes red from weeping, they beat their breasts and wailed in sorrow, calling out the names of their slain husbands, sons and fathers. Hearing those pitiful cries, people thought the time of universal destruction had arrived.

The Pandavas with Yudhisthira at their head followed in chariots along with Dhritarastra and Sanjaya. Krishna rode with Arjuna. Numerous sages headed by Dhaumya and Narada walked alongside the procession, reciting sacred chants. Arriving at the river, they offered sacraments for the fallen warriors. When the ceremonies were complete and the Pandavas had taken their ritual bath in the Ganges, Krishna and the sages consoled them by explaining the transcendental wisdom of the Vedas.

(8:5-15) Krishna said, "Do not lament! All these heroes have attained higher regions of enduring happiness. None in this world can avoid death, and for a warrior there is no better way to die than at the edge of weapons."

A few days later, Krishna met privately with the five Pandavas and Draupadi. "My dear Yudhisthira," he said, "I am pleased to see you again ruling as the emperor of the world."

With a sorrowful heart, Yudhisthira replied, "We have all paid heavily for my ambition!"

Krishna consolingly put his arm on Yudhisthira's shoulder. "You are not to blame for these warriors' deaths." Turning to Draupadi, he continued, "They condemned themselves to death on that fateful day when they insulted this chaste lady."

Seeing Yudhisthira still morose, Krishna added, "Nevertheless, if you fear the sin of killing your relatives, you can perform three horse sacrifices." Embracing the brothers, and offering Draupadi blessings, Krishna then left to see the sages headed by Vyasadeva before departing for Dvaraka. Later that day, the Lord ascended his chariot, accompanied by Satyaki and Uddhava. The five Pandavas, along with the women in their family, stood next to it. Suddenly, six fiery Brahmastra missiles descended on the party. One headed for each of the Pandavas who hurriedly drew their swords in a futile gesture of self-defence. The sixth missile targeted Uttara who was at the time heavily pregnant with Arjuna's grandchild.

In great terror, Uttara at once called out to Krishna, "O Supreme Lord! Master of the universe! If you desire my death I do not mind, but please save my embryo!"

Seeing the danger facing his devotees, Krishna released his Sudarshana disc to protect the five brothers. Simultaneously, as the Supersoul in the heart, he personally covered Uttara's embryo, shielding both the unborn child and his young mother from the devastating effect of the Brahmastra.

When the dreadful glare of the weapons subsided, Uttara collapsed in a faint. Draupadi, Kunti and the five Pandava brothers hastily gathered around her, fearing that she and her child had been killed. Relieved to see symptoms of life, they looked up at Krishna in bewilderment. What had just happened? Krishna reassured them. "This was the work of Ashvatthama intending to destroy your lineage. Do not worry, Uttara will soon recover, and her child is unharmed. As for Ashvatthama, he has exhausted the last of his power and does not pose any further threat."

(8.17-18) Shaken by the unexpected attack, the elderly Kunti slowly rose from Uttara's side and unsteadily approached the Lord. Folding her hands and with tears of love streaming from her eyes, Kunti knelt beside the chariot on which Krishna stood and lowered her head to the ground to offer obeisance. With a look of alarm on his face, Krishna jumped down from his chariot and gently raised her. "Aunt Kunti, what are you doing? There is no need for you to show me such respect. You are my superior!"

Kunti spoke in a choked voice. "My dear Krishna, I offer my respects to you because you are the original personality and are unaffected by the qualities of the material world."

"My dear Aunt," objected Krishna, "I am simply your nephew!"

(8:19-22) Kunti shook her head. "You are the invisible Supersoul of all existence, residing within and without. Though you control everything, ignorant people do not understand this, just as a child does not see the puppeteer moving puppets. Even the liberated sages find it hard to perfectly know you, so what to speak of a simple woman like me."

Aunt and nephew stood looking tenderly at one another, as Kunti continued, "Though you are the original Supreme Lord, you have come as the son of my brother, Vasudeva, giving joy to his wife, Devaki. The cowherd Nanda and his wife Yashoda are even more blessed, because they raised you and were able to relish your pastoral pastimes in Vrindavan."

Kunti stroked Krishna's face with motherly affection. "I offer my respectful obeisance to you, dear Lord, whose eyes resemble lotus petals, who are always decorated with a lotus garland, whose navel resembles a lotus flower and whose feet are marked with lotuses."

(8:23-24) Kunti again knelt and placed her head at Krishna's feet, but Krishna once more lifted her and she went on speaking.

"You rescued your own mother only once when you released her from Kamsa's prison. You have shown me, your widowed aunt, even more mercy, for you saved me and my sons repeatedly from a series of dangers."

Remembering the many threats she had faced, and how the Lord had always rescued her, Kunti wept.

"You protected Bhima from certain death when the evil-minded Duryodhana fed him poisoned food. Then, by your grace alone, we survived Duryodhana's plot to burn us to death in our sleep."

Kunti shuddered as she remembered that fearful night in Varanavata; how after escaping from the blazing house, they raced through the dark and perilous forest in fear of their lives.

"Without your protection, how could we have survived the attacks of the fearsome cannibals, Baka and Hidimba, and the other hardships we faced whilst living in the wilderness. Then came the great battle. Duryodhana's army was far superior to ours. His generals were unconquerable. Yet, thanks to you, my sons emerged victorious. And now you have miraculously saved us yet again from Ashvatthama's deadly Brahmastra missiles."

"You and your sons are now safe," Krishna reassured her. "Your trials are over."

(8:25-27) "I do not mind any of the difficulties we have endured. Indeed, I wish all those calamities would happen again and again; so that we could see you again and again, for by seeing you we will no longer see repeated births and deaths."

Kunti continued in earnest tones. "O Krishna! A distressed person sincerely turns to you, thinking he has no other shelter. The materially successful, however, proud of their wealth, learning or social position, cannot feelingly call out to you. Therefore, out of kindness, you put your devotee in difficulty; for only those who approach you in a mood of total dependence can attract your full mercy."

Folding her hands and bowing her head, Kunti said, "I offer you my respects. You give yourself to those devotees who love you without material motive. You have nothing to do with those interested in worldly gain, but you are so kind to your servants that you forgive them even if they inadvertently offend you. You will even fulfil the desires of devotees who seek liberation.

(8:28-31) "In your form as eternal Time you always destroy those who offend your devotees. You are the original supreme controller, without beginning or end, existing everywhere. You are equal to all, giving everyone the results of their own acts."

"I have many detractors who would disagree with you, my dear aunt," said Krishna, with a smile.

Kunti shook her head, saddened by people's ignorance. "No one can truly understand your human-like pastimes, as much as they try. Certainly, you neither favour nor envy anyone, and only in ignorance do people think otherwise."

Kunti wiped her tears with the end of her sari as she went speaking. "O soul of the universe, why should anyone expect to perfectly understand you? You never take a material birth nor engage in material acts, yet you repeatedly appear in different forms and act in so many ways. Truly this is hard to understand. I am simply bewildered when I think how your mother, Yashoda, bound you with rope when you misbehaved. Although fear personified fears you, seeing Yashoda angry, you were afraid. Tears flooded your eyes, smearing your black mascara."

(8:32-36) Kunti shook her head in amazement. "I have heard sages discuss your activities. Some argue that you came to establish Yudhisthira as the emperor. Others say you appeared in the Yadu dynasty to glorify your devotee, King Yadu.

"Still others say you came because Vasudeva and Devaki prayed for you to deliver them and your other devotees from the vicious and atheistic miscreants; while some sages say you came to save the world on Lord Brahma's request.

"I have also heard it said the real reason you have come to enact so many mystifying pastimes is to inspire people to hear and talk about you. One attracted to such discussions gains immediate relief from sufferings arising from past misdeeds. Even the very sinful can attain pure love for you by regularly discussing your glories. Indeed, those who take pleasure in narrations of your transcendental activities will certainly see your lotus-like feet, which alone can free one from the cycle of birth and death."

(8:37-40) Kunti began to tremble with ecstatic emotion. As she swayed back and forth, Krishna placed an arm around her to steady her. He called to the royal attendants. "Quickly bring water!"

Sipping cool water from a silver cup, Kunti gradually regained her composure. Krishna embraced his aunt, and then touching her feet asked permission to depart.

"I have been here for many months and I am receiving messages from my father that I am needed back in Dvaraka," he explained.

Kunti became agitated. "Dear Krishna! Please do not go. Whatever you need to do in Dvaraka, you can accomplish merely by your desire. Why do you wish to leave us, who so completely depend on you? You know my sons have created many enemies after the war. You are our only shelter!"

"My dear Aunt," replied Krishna soothingly, "you have no need to fear. Yudhisthira is protected by his virtue. Your other sons are also powerful, and we Yadus are your stalwart political allies."

Kunti again shook her head. "As the senses have no power when the soul leaves the body, similarly neither my sons nor the Yadus have any power when you are not with us."

She clutched Krishna's hands in her own and pleaded, "My Lord, please do not go! Only because your footprints mark this land does it appear beautiful. When you leave, it will no longer be so. This thriving earth, filled with herbs, fruit-laden trees, forests, mountains and rivers only prospers because of your glance."

(8:41-43) Kunti's mind drifted to thoughts of her brother Vasudeva and his wife Devaki. Surely they must be suffering in Krishna's absence. Maybe he should go to them, but if Krishna left, what would happen to her sons?

"O Krishna! Because of my dual attachment to both the Pandavas and the Yadavas, I am feeling torn. Please sever my material affections. O Lord of the Madhu dynasty, just as the Ganges forever flows to the sea without hindrance, please let my attraction be constantly drawn to you alone."

Kunti sank to her knees with her hands clasped. "O Krishna! Friend of Arjuna! Best of the Yadavas! Destroyer of the vicious kings! Lord of undiminished strength! Protector of the cows, brahmins and devotees! Master of yogic powers! Guru of all! O almighty God! I offer you my humble obeisance!"

(8:44-52) Krishna bent over and gently helped his aunt to rise. Wiping away her tears, he assured her that her desire would be fulfilled and her attraction would never waver from him. Then he turned to address Yudhisthira.

"O king, before I leave, I must bid farewell to the other ladies in the palace."

Draupadi and Subhadra had gone into the palace to tend to Uttara who was still weak from her ordeal. Krishna, Yudhisthira, Kunti, Satyaki and Uddhava walked back to the palace, followed by the other Pandavas. The Lord entered the women's quarters to enquire after Uttara and found her in bed surrounded by anxious female relatives and friends.

The Lord said to them, "Do not fear for Uttara or her child. They will both be fine. Indeed, Uttara will give birth to a son who will grow up to be a great monarch."

After exchanging affectionate words with Uttara, Draupadi and Subhadra, he tenderly bid them farewell. He then left, followed by the Pandavas, Satyaki and Uddhava. Turning to Yudhisthira and said, "O king, my relatives in Dvaraka want me to return. Please allow me to depart."

Yudhisthira's face contorted into a mask of pain. Placing a hand on Krishna's arm he said, "Surely you will return to Dvaraka if it is your will, but how will I survive without your guidance?"

In doleful tones, Yudhisthira confided his fears. Ashvatthama's recent attack had highlighted the extent of enmity the war had created. There would be much work to do to strengthen alliances, and to ensure the millions of widows and orphans were all protected. The road ahead seemed overwhelming.

Krishna encouraged him. "My dear Yudhisthira, the time has come. You must now accept the throne."

Overcome by emotion, Yudhisthira shook his head. "Surely I am unfit to rule the world. How can I lead anyone? I am the most sinful man! Just see my heart, so full of ignorance! Just to further the interests of my own body, which is fit to be eaten by jackals, I have killed legions of family and friends. For my sake, boys, brahmins, well-wishers, friends, parents, preceptors and brothers have perished. I shall have to suffer in hell for millions of years for my sins!"

Yudhisthira turned to Bhima and said, "Brother, take the throne. I shall go to the forest to perform penance."

Bhima looked shocked. "My lord, this can never be. How can I rule in your place? Do not censure yourself so. You are a great warrior and leader. You have done your duty. Now accept the throne and rule over this wide earth."

Yudhisthira said nothing. Arjuna came up to him and placed a hand on his shoulder. "How have you spoken such words, dear brother? After conquering your enemies, you are now the world's rightful ruler. As a *kshatriya*, it is your duty to protect the people. It is not time for you to renounce. Kings like you must perform sacrifice and then distribute wealth to those in need. In this way, pious monarchs increase their virtue and fame. The world stands in need of a leader. Following in the footsteps of the great kings in our line, you should become emperor of the earth. How could you accept any other path?"

Yudhisthira sighed. "There is no sin for a king who kills enemies who attack his people. Duryodhana, however, posed no threat to the citizens. I have killed him and his supporters only out of greed for a kingdom."

Nakula said, "My lord, by performing your kingly duties you can absolve yourself of any sin you may have incurred."

Yudhisthira lowered his head. "No amount of material welfare work can counteract the suffering I have caused by this war."

Sahadeva also tried to convince the king. "By performing horse sacrifices, as Krishna suggested, you can purify yourself, my lord."

Yudhisthira looked around at his brothers, who were all gazing anxiously at him. He spoke in a low, anguished voice. "Just as one cannot purify muddy water by straining it through mud, nor a wine-stained pot by washing it with wine, similarly it is not possible to counteract the killing of men by sacrificing animals."

Krishna said, "Yudhisthira, your brothers have sacrificed much to win your kingdom back. You cannot desert them now. They and the people need you. Do not shy away from your duty!"

Yudhisthira turned his tear-filled eyes toward Krishna. Seeing the Lord's beautiful features and hearing his instruction calmed his mind. He spoke pleadingly. "O Krishna! Please delay your return to Dvaraka for a little longer. My heart is burning! I cannot see my way forward!"

Krishna embraced Yudhisthira. "Obliged by your love for me, I shall stay a few more days."

***

When Suta stopped speaking, no sound could be heard. Along with the sages, it seemed as if even the birds, fire and air were listening silently.

After a few moments, Shaunaka broke the silence. "What an enthralling account. I noted that Queen Kunti shed light on our third question regarding why Krishna appears. He mainly comes to perform his wonderful pastimes so conditioned souls can take delight in hearing about and discussing him."[29.]

Suta's eyes lit up. "Yes, I was also stressing this earlier. Such discussions awaken our attraction for Krishna, thereby destroying our illusion."

"What happened to the child in Uttara's womb?"

"He was born in good health and later became the great Emperor Parikit. When the incident with Ashvatthama occurred, the embryonic child saw Lord Krishna, club in hand, encircling and protecting him.

From that moment, he was devoted to Krishna, and all through his life he would scan each face he saw, searching for that person he had seen in the womb. For this reason, he was called 'Parikit'—'the seeker'."

The sages expressed wonderment that Krishna had appeared to the unborn child in his mother's womb and protected him from harm.

(8:16) Suta laughed. "O brahmins, do not think this to be especially wonderful for Krishna. Merely by his will, he creates, maintains and annihilates the universe."

Shaunaka wondered how a sober monarch like Yudhisthira could become so affected by material grief that he would consider abandoning his duty. Revealing this doubt to Suta he added, "Only an ignorant person thinks of violence and nonviolence in terms of the body. How was the emperor so bewildered?"

Suta replied, "Yudhisthira is a self-realised soul. Krishna directly induced his confusion."

Shaunaka frowned. "How can that be? Krishna himself tried without success to dissipate his grief and bewilderment."

"The Lord did this to glorify Bhishma," explained Suta. "He confounded Yudhisthira's mind, making the king incapable of understanding even his instructions, because the Lord wanted to give Bhishma the credit for enlightening Yudhisthira. Krishna also wanted to please Bhishma by visiting him along with the Pandavas."

"Please tell us what happened when they saw Bhishma."

"Listen," said Suta.

9. Bhishma Departs

At Krishna's behest King Yudhisthira receives instructions from the mighty warrior, Bhishma, who then leaves this world in Krishna's presence.

(9:1-9) Resplendent like Kuvera, the heavenly treasurer, Yudhisthira rode on a great golden chariot, yoked to sixteen white horses. His brothers rode behind him on equally magnificent conveyances. Krishna accompanied Arjuna on his chariot. Great sages and brahmins, including Vyasadeva and Dhaumya, walked alongside them as they steadily made their way to where grandfather Bhishma lay on his bed of arrows. Bhishma was attended by many elite sages including Parashurama, Vasishtha, Gautama, and Shukadeva, who were reciting the Lord's glories. Nearby also sat his old friend Kripacharya.

(9:10-11) Hearing the thunderous sounds of their approaching chariots, the sages rose and made way for the Pandavas and Krishna to approach Bhishma. On seeing the Lord, Bhishma was overwhelmed with gratitude. Turning to Kripacharya, he said, "Just see the wonderful causeless mercy of

Lord Krishna! I am most unfortunate. I have no qualification. I opposed Krishna's most intimate friend, Arjuna—I even tried to kill him! Still, the Lord, who is worshipped by all great sages, is so kind and merciful that he has come to see an abominable person like me at the last point of my life."[29]

Yudhisthira was grief-stricken to see his beloved grandfather in such a pained condition. Blaming himself, he offered his respects and sat meekly to one side along with his brothers. Seeing Bhishma's pitiable condition, Krishna forgot himself in his compassion. Tears flowed from his eyes as he gently greeted the fallen hero. With great difficulty Bhishma placed his two palms together, and joyfully said, "O Krishna! My Lord! Lord of the Universe! I offer you my worship!"

By virtue of Krishna's presence, the pain left Bhishma's body and his mind became calm. Krishna affectionately told Bhishma that his grandsons had come to see him. "Yudhisthira feels too ashamed to present himself to you. He blames himself for this war."

Bhishma turned his head slowly and saw the Pandavas sitting with bowed heads. In a voice choked with affection, Bhishma called out, "Come. Come. My beloved grandsons! Let me congratulate you on your glorious victory."

(9:12) The brothers knelt on either side of their grandfather. They each tearfully begged for his forgiveness.

"There is nothing to forgive," said Bhishma. "Since your childhood, you good souls have continuously suffered terrible injustices. The war was not your fault. It was the only way to re-establish justice. Your behaviour has been above reproach. Indeed, it is because of your piety that you brothers have always been protected by the brahmins, God, and religion itself.

(9:13) Bhishma closed his eyes, remembering the day the orphaned Pandavas first reached Hastinapura with their young widowed mother, Kunti. After Pandu's death, the sages escorted them to their ancestral home. Tears ran from the corners of his eyes as he recalled the hardships Kunti had undergone due to the malicious intrigues of Dhritarastra's eldest son, Duryodhana, and his maternal uncle, Shakuni. The Pandavas also remembered the various plots to kill them. Duryodhana had not even been pacified when his father gave him half the kingdom. Burning with envy to see the Pandavas prosper, he plotted to cheat them of their half, and went on to humiliate them by dishonouring their wife.

"Poor Kunti," Bhishma said, "I saw how much she suffered because of the gambling match."

(9:14-17) Yudhisthira hung his head in shame remembering how he had staked first his brothers, then himself, and finally the chaste and sinless Draupadi. His chest heaved with emotion, and his face flushed as he castigated himself.

"What a wretched person I am! How many sins I must have performed in my previous lives."

Bhishma reassured him. "Do not blame yourself, Yudhisthira. You are not at fault for what has happened. Indeed, you are the emblem of piety. Everything was arranged by inexorable Time, under whose control everyone is carried, just as the wind carries clouds. Otherwise, how could you have suffered so much, even though you are the son of the god of religion, protected by the mighty Bhima and the powerful Arjuna, and above all, Lord Krishna? Yudhisthira, know that Time is identical with the Lord, and all this has happened by his desire."

Yudhisthira turned his tear-stained face toward Bhishma. "O grandfather, if everything happened by the Lord's will, then what is his intent?"

Bhishma's chuckle turned into a painful cough and he spat out blood. With difficulty he replied, "O king, no one can ascertain the Lord's plan, not even the great gods, Shiva and Brahma. Even the sages' exhaustive philosophical enquiries cannot divine the Lord's purposes. There is no point in asking such a question. Better to just abide by his orders without argument."

Yudhisthira's brow furrowed. "What does the Lord want me to do? Should I go to the forest and perform penance, or stay in Hastinapura and rule the kingdom?"

"Why are you confused, Yudhisthira? His order is clear. You must unhesitatingly accept the responsibility of ruling and protecting your citizens."

"How can I be sure that this is his desire?"

Bhishma's eyes turned toward Krishna who was next to Yudhisthira. "Because the Supreme Lord sits beside you even as we speak, and he has repeatedly instructed you to assume the throne."

Yudhisthira turned his head toward Krishna sitting next to him. His cousin Krishna was the Supreme Lord? He turned back to Bhishma with a look of bafflement.

(9:18) "Do not be so surprised, Yudhisthira!" Bhishma smiled. "Krishna mystifies everyone. Those who want to enjoy separately from him are deluded by his external energy to forget his supreme position. His devotees who love him, on the other hand, are bewildered by his internal potency, and thus forget his supreme position."

The sun's rays shone directly on Krishna's serene face, enhancing his beauty, as he looked lovingly at his many devotees. The sages present sang mantras of glorification. The five brothers, however, looked again and again at Krishna and then at Bhishma. They knew Krishna was wonderful, but how could he be the Supreme Lord? He was their dear most friend, their cousin and confidante.

Bhishma fixed his tear-filled eyes on Krishna's face. "This Krishna is none other than the inconceivable, original Personality of Godhead. He is the first Narayana, the supreme enjoyer. Yet he moves amongst the Vrishni family as if he were a mere mortal like us. He thus baffles us all."

Yudhisthira gazed at Krishna. It must be as grandfather Bhishma says. He is renowned for his learning, virtue and spiritual wisdom. Why then would Krishna have put them into so much difficulty? He turned back to Bhishma with a quizzical expression.

(9:19-21) "Your confusion does not surprise me," said Bhishma. "Krishna reveals his will only to great spiritual authorities such as Shiva, Narada, and his own incarnation, Sage Kapila. My dear son, Yudhisthira, you must understand that Krishna puts his beloved devotees, like you, into difficulty, only to deepen your loving exchanges with him. Do you remember how you turned to him repeatedly when calamities came? Thinking he was your maternal cousin, you sought his friendship and counsel. You asked him to become your messenger and ally. He always reciprocated with you because of your great love for him."

(9:22-24) Bhishma looked toward Krishna. "You show your kindness to everyone if they have full faith in your protection. Because I am such an unflinching devotee, you have come here at the last moment of my life to give me your audience."

"Grandfather," said Yudhisthira, "please tell me the means by which one can become the Lord's pure devotee and thereby enjoy his shelter."

Bhishma replied, "At the time of death, Krishna will appear in the minds of those who always chant his holy names with fixed attention. Thus, the karmic reactions that kept them bound in material existence will be destroyed."

Bhishma turned to Krishna. "My Lord, please appear before me as the four-handed Narayana. I wish to see this glorious form as I leave my body."

(9:25-28) Krishna placed his hand over Bhishma's, then he turned to Yudhisthira and nodded, indicating Yudhisthira should continue asking his grandfather his other questions.

Yudhisthira began by asking about the essential principles of statecraft. Bhishma then explained the moral duties of society in two divisions. One was for those desiring material enjoyment and the other for those more inclined to renunciation. He said that everyone should be trained to be charitable. He also described the specific duties of the king, of women, of devotees, and of each of the different occupations, supporting his explanations with scriptural evidence.

(9:29-31) Over the course of the many days that Bhishma instructed Yudhisthira, the sun gradually moved to the northern hemisphere. Noting this, Bhishma, who was able to die at a time of his own choosing, told Yudhisthira, "My dear king, the auspicious time for my departure has arrived. I have spoken of many things, and I have fought many battles. Now I desire to fix my mind on Lord Krishna in preparation for death."

As Yudhisthira bowed his head in acquiescence, Bhishma gazed at Krishna. The Lord, manifesting his splendid four-armed form as Narayana, stood before him dressed in yellow garments and adorned with numerous jewels. Preparing to leave his body, Bhishma began to glorify Krishna.

(9:32-34) "At the end of my life, I desire to exclusively fix my thoughts on you, Lord, the creator of the material world. Although you are fully self-satisfied, you sometimes descend here to perform your pleasure pastimes with your pure devotees."

Recollecting how attractive Krishna looked on the battlefield of Kurukshetra, Bhishma said, "As you drove your friend's chariot, the sun rays made your outfit glitter and shine, and your hair which had turned ashen because of the dust raised by the horses, flew behind you in the wind. Even though your body was covered by wounds inflicted by my sharp arrows, and sweat poured from your brow, you did not abandon your dear friend, Arjuna."

(9:35-39) Casting his mind back to the first day of the war, Bhishma continued, "On Arjuna's request, you took his chariot to the middle of the battlefield. By glancing over the soldiers in Duryodhana's army, you shortened their lives merely by your will. Then when Arjuna became bewildered, you spoke transcendental knowledge to dispel his doubts. O Lord, may my mind always be attracted to you."

Bhishma became increasingly absorbed in remembering Krishna's many favours toward his devotees. He recalled how, during the battle, Krishna sacrificed his own promise not to fight, in order to keep Bhishma's vow that he would force the Lord to fight in order to save his friend Arjuna.

"You rushed at me in anger, as a lion attacks an elephant," Bhishma recalled, with a chuckle. "Your shield was broken and your body smeared with blood from wounds inflicted by my arrows. O Krishna! I desire to always behold your beautiful form driving Arjuna's chariot, anxious to protect him by all means. All the warriors who died on the battlefield attained your eternal kingdom simply because of seeing your attractive features."

(9:40-49) Desiring to attain their blessings, Bhishma remembered Krishna's dearest devotees, the gopis of Vrindavan. "You danced and joked with them as equals!" he marveled.

"In truth, no one is your equal. You are the Supreme Personality of Godhead. All the great sages, gods, and kings of the world acknowledged this truth about you during Yudhisthira's Rajasuya sacrifice.

"Some people think the Supreme Lord is impersonal, all-pervasive energy known as Brahman, and others think the Supreme is the Supersoul in the hearts of all living beings. Because I have transcended all material duality, I can see that you are the one Supreme Lord. Brahman and the Supersoul are simply your different aspects, just as the sunshine and the sun disc are aspects of the sun god."

Bhishma fell silent. Focusing his eyes and mind on Krishna's form standing before him, he left for the spiritual world.

When Bhishma's body became limp and lifeless, the sages and kings present observed a moment's silence in his honour. The gods began to shower flowers from the heavens, and the kings joined with the celestials in praising Bhishma with instruments and song.

After performing Bhishma's last rites and watching as his body was burned on a great bier swathed in garlands, Yudhisthira was momentarily overcome with grief. He stood motionless, gazing at the smoking remains of Bhishma's body. As he slowly turned to leave he saw Kripacharya standing at a distance. Yudhisthira, followed by Krishna, approached his old teacher, who lowered his head in shame.

"Forgive me, Yudhisthira," said Kripacharya. "Following Ashvatthama's orders I have grievously wronged you. I shall now go to the mountains to perform penance."

Yudhisthira reached down to touch his teacher's feet, but Kripacharya stopped him and raised him up.

"My lord," said Yudhisthira, "do not censure yourself. Everything happens by the supreme will. Pray return to Hastinapura with me. I will need your wise counsel to rebuild this vast kingdom."

Krishna also spoke reassuringly. "Yudhisthira is right. Besides which, your presence in Hastinapura will provide much consolation to the bereaved Dhritarastra and Gandhari."

With a deep sigh, Kripacharya agreed. When the sages departed for their hermitages he returned to Hastinapura with Yudhisthira.

Always taking great care to comfort his distraught uncle, Dhritarastra, and his aunt, Gandhari, Yudhisthira began to rule the kingdom with Dhritarastra and Krishna's approval.

10. Krishna Returns Home

After installing Yudhisthira as the world's emperor, Krishna departs for Dwaraka. The ladies of Hastinapura praise him as he leaves.

(10:1-8) Shaunaka asked about Yudhisthira's reign as emperor. "Surely, he could not have ruled with a peaceful mind, after so many of his family members had been slain?"

Suta said, "The great king Yudhisthira lived only to satisfy Krishna, who was pleased to see him assume the throne. Thus, in a mood of service, and assisted by his brothers, he happily accepted his rightful position as king."

Suta described how Yudhisthira restored the Kurus' fortunes, which had been devastated by the war. Under his righteous rule, the earth became opulent like the heavens. The people were free from disturbance and there were no natural disasters. Because the king satisfied Krishna, the gods were pleased, and everything flourished."

"Did Krishna remain with him?" asked Shaunaka.

"He stayed in Hastinapura for a few months to console his grieving friends and relations, especially his sister Subhadra. Finally, with Yudhisthira's permission, he departed for Dvaraka."

"I expect this would have caused more grief for Hastinapura's residents than the war itself," said Shaunaka. "Please describe to us the scene of his departure and of his arrival in Dvaraka."

Suta continued his narration.

***

(10:9-36) Hearing the Lord was leaving, the palace residents fell into confusion. Krishna was their very life. How could they face his separation? Subhadra, Draupadi, Kunti, the Pandavas, Kripacharya, Dhaumya, and all the other citizens of Hastinapura stopped whatever they were doing when the news reached them. They moved about in bewilderment, unable to do anything.

"I surely cannot live without him," Yudhisthira declared to his brothers. "Even one who has only heard about the Lord's glorious qualities can never stop thinking about him. What to speak of we who have become accustomed to eat, sit, rest and speak with him in person."

Remembering their many exchanges with Krishna, and anticipating his separation, the five brothers became restless.

On the day of the Lord's departure, the city streets were lined with hundreds of thousands of anxious citizens, all desiring a last glimpse of the Lord. As he proceeded slowly along the road, they gazed at him with unblinking eyes. Arjuna stood on his chariot holding a jeweled parasol over his head, while Uddhava and Satyaki cooled him with ornate fans. Yudhisthira had his great army accompany Krishna. Drums, trumpets, bells, lutes, conches and many other instruments sounded as the majestic procession moved along the broad paved road. Brahmins chanted melodic Sanskrit prayers bestowing blessings. The Lord graciously accepted his devotees' services with affectionate smiles and glances.

The royal ladies tried to stem their tears, which they feared might cause misfortune. The other ladies of Hastinapura rushed out onto their high balconies. In their haste they did not dress properly. Their hearts beat rapidly as Krishna passed by with his entourage. None of them could take their eyes away from him. They showered him with flowers and sang his glories.

One lady said, "Here is that original Supreme Person who existed before the creation, and into whom all beings will merge at the end. He is known only by pure-hearted devotees who steadily serve him with mind and senses controlled."

As the stately procession moved slowly past them another lady said, "Dear friends, there is the Supreme Personality whose attractive pastimes are described by his pure devotees in exalted writings. He creates, maintains and annihilates the material world and yet remains unaffected."

Forgetting their duties, even those of serving their husbands and caring for their children, the ladies crowded the rooftops along the highway. They jostled each other in perplexity, trying to get a better view of the Lord. Praising the good fortune of the residents of Krishna's kingdom, one of them said, "Oh, how glorious is King Yadu's dynasty, and how virtuous is Mathura, where the supreme leader of all living beings, the husband of the goddess of fortune, took birth and played in his childhood."

Another lady added, "Dvaraka's inhabitants are supremely fortunate. They always see the soul of all beings in his loving feature. And just think of his wives, whose hands he accepted. How they must have undergone vows, austerities, sacrifices and perfect worship of the Lord to be receiving his conjugal embraces and kisses. The Vrindavan damsels would faint just by imagining such favours."

Krishna smiled and glanced up at them, finding their simple, heartfelt words more pleasing than the perfectly composed Vedic mantras recited by the brahmins. As they caught the Lord's eye, the ladies almost swooned in ecstasy.

The procession passed the love-struck ladies and gradually left the city. The Pandavas accompanied the Lord for a considerable distance, unable to face the prospect of parting. Krishna finally persuaded them to return, whilst he continued to Dvaraka, passing through many countries where the residents came out in their thousands to see him.

11. The Glories of Dvaraka

Krishna arrives in Dvaraka and is greeted by his citizens and family members.

(11:1-5) When Krishna reached the outskirts of Dvaraka, he blew his conch to herald his arrival. The plump white shell, gripped by Krishna's graceful hand, appeared reddened by the touch of his ruby lips. It looked like a white swan playing among red lotuses. Hearing that sound, which strikes fear into fear personified, the citizens ran out to greet him like joyful children greeting their long absent father. As if offering a lamp to the sun, they made presentations of gifts to the Lord while reciting prayers and praises.

(11:6-16) The citizens said, "Self-sufficient and fully satisfied within yourself, you are worshipped by the best of gods and are the final goal of life. You are the supreme transcendent Lord, untouched by time."

They praised Krishna as their father, mother, spiritual master, and venerable deity. Feeling greatly blessed to see him, they expressed their heartfelt affection. "You rarely visit even the celestials, but today we can see your smiling face and all-auspicious spiritual form."

They lamented that when he was away, the days dragged unbearably, with every moment seeming like a million years. "At that time our eyes are useless, as if bereft of sunlight. How can we survive in your absence?"

Glancing benevolently over the citizens, Krishna entered the city which displayed the opulence of all seasons, with flower gardens, orchards, lotus-filled lakes, and delightful ashrams. Countless flags and festoons adorned the buildings, and gateways and arches were decorated with colourful signs and garlands. Scented water was sprinkled on the spotless roads. Flowers, rice and seeds were decoratively strewn about. In every doorway stood auspicious items such as pots of yoghurt, milk and water, as well as fruits, sugarcane, and candles. Billows of fragrant incense smoke wafted throughout the city. Noting all of this, Krishna smiled with pleasure.

(11:17-33) The Lord's relatives came out to greet him on golden chariots, like a stream of gods issuing from Amaravati. Along with them came effulgent brahmins clad in simple loincloths, and intoning sacred hymns. Musical instruments sounded while dancers, dramatists and singers made impromptu performances depicting Krishna's pastimes. Beautiful ladies sat behind veils in their jewelled carriages, smiling shyly as he passed.

Krishna got down from his chariot to greet everyone according to their status. To some, he showed respect by bowing his head. Others, he embraced. With some, he shook hands, and to others he offered benedictions. The Lord respectfully greeted representatives of all the social orders. Surrounded by joyous citizens singing his praises, he walked toward his palace, his head protected from the bright sun by a white parasol. Proceeding gracefully along the road, his dark body adorned with yellow garments, he was fanned on either side with white yak-tail fans, and showered with flower petals. It appeared as if the sun, moon, lightning and rainbows simultaneously surrounded a dark cloud.

Krishna then entered the vast marble palace where his father Vasudeva lived with his sixteen wives. They shed tears of joy to see Krishna, and he respectfully placed his head at their feet, one by one, beginning with his father. His mother Devaki sat the Lord on her lap and milk flowed from her breasts out of affection. After taking permission from Vasudeva, the Lord left and then simultaneously entered his 16,108 palaces, expanding himself into that many forms.

When each of Krishna's queens saw him arrive, they stood up quickly. Though they wanted to immediately run to him, out of feminine shyness they checked themselves. Covering their charming faces with the ends of their silk saris, they looked about bashfully. When they caught the Lord's glance, they each embraced him within their hearts and then sent their sons forward to physically embrace him. Despite themselves, they shed tears, overwhelmed with emotion. The Lord smiled at them, reciprocating their pure love. Speaking gentle words of affection, he entered his inner quarters with each of his wives and rested for the night, satisfied that his mission of killing the miscreants was complete.

***

Suta paused in his narration to take a sip of water. Shaunaka sat in silent thought for some moments. Hearing how Krishna was happy that the wrongdoers had been slain, he again wondered about the Lord's neutrality and asked Suta to explain it further.

(11:34-36) Suta said, "Krishna is equally disposed to all. He merely reciprocates with our desires. Those who wish to aggressively expand their material power and influence are brought together by the Lord's arrangement. They thus fight and destroy one another. Krishna takes no part in such conflicts. He is like the wind which causes friction between bamboo stalks and so sparks a fire."

"Is this because Krishna has no material desires?" asked Shaunaka.

"Exactly," replied Suta.

"How is it then that he enjoys with his wives? He seems to be affected by lust just like an ordinary man."

"Could any normal person expand himself into more than 16,000 forms, each acting differently with each of his wives? Krishna was merely reciprocating with their desires to have him as their husband. Although they were the most beautiful women in creation, and although they tried to allure him with furtive glances, coy smiles and feminine gestures which could overcome even Shiva himself, the Lord was never agitated. Indeed, Cupid threw down his flower bow in frustration, unable to even slightly disturb the Lord's mind with his arrows of passion."

"How fortunate were those ladies to have such intimate association with Krishna," said Shaunaka. "Can anyone become his wife?"

"Yes, but it requires complete surrender to the Lord. As the women of Hastinapura said, his wives must have performed devotional service over so many lifetimes. They were imbued with *prema*, which alone can attract Krishna."

(11:37-39) "Why is it that the Lord's loving exchanges with his wives so much resemble worldly dealings?" asked Shaunaka, knowing that many would find this difficult to comprehend.

"Only fools think this way, my friend," said Suta. "Because they compare the Lord to themselves, they cannot understand that he is never affected by lust. Consider this for a moment: whoever takes shelter of the Lord becomes completely detached from worldly enjoyment. How then can material pleasures attract the Lord?"

Shaunaka asked about Krishna's wives. "From what you say, it seems they were mistaken in thinking Krishna was attached to them. Since they are pure devotees, how can they be in such ignorance?"

"This is a different kind of ignorance," said Suta, with a laugh. "Just as the atheists cannot understand the Lord, so, too, are his pure devotees bewildered. Their confusion, however, is induced by the Lord's spiritual potency to facilitate loving exchanges with him. It is entirely different from the ignorance of materialistic people which is caused by lust. Though the Lord is never controlled by anyone, his wives' innocent belief that they controlled him with their love gave him immense pleasure."

The sages sat spellbound. They had simply expected to hear about the reason for Parikit's renunciation and his meeting with Shukadeva. To illustrate King Parikit's high devotional status, Suta had begun by explaining how Krishna had saved him while still in his mother's womb. Due to devotional ecstasy, Suta had unexpectedly recounted Kunti's prayers, Bhishma's passing away, and Krishna's return to Dvaraka.

12. Parikit Born

Parikit's vision whilst in his mother's womb. At his birth, astrologers describe his illustrious future.

(12:1-6) Eager to return to Parikit's history, Shaunaka said, "Please tell us how Krishna protected the unborn Parikit from the unstoppable Brahmastra. Why did that great monarch die in the prime of his life? Also, pray tell us his destination after death. Since Shukadeva chose to speak the *Srimad Bhagavatam* to him, we are intrigued to know more about him."

"To properly comprehend Parikit's greatness," replied Suta, "one must understand the position of his grandfather, Yudhisthira. Although his opulence and power were so extensive that even the celestials envied him, Yudhisthira had no attachment to worldly enjoyment. Like his father Pandu, his mind was always fixed on Krishna's service and he wielded his imperial power without personal ambition. Due to his great love for Krishna, he was blessed with a most exalted grandson, Parikit."

Suta picked up Parikit's story from the moment when Ashvatthama's Brahmastra scorched him while he was still in his mother's womb.

***

(12:7-14) As the unborn child was being scorched by the searing heat of the Brahmastra, he saw a small form coming to his aid. His rescuer had four powerful arms, a beautiful blackish complexion, and his eyes were blood red with fury. Dressed in yellow garments, adorned with a brilliant golden helmet and earrings,. he encircled the embryo like a shooting star. Constantly whirling his club, he neutralised the Brahmastra's radiation. When the weapon's glare had subsided, he stopped moving. The baby could now more clearly see the charming features of his benefactor, who smiled briefly at him and then disappeared. From that moment on, he constantly wondered about the identity of the mysterious hero who had saved him from certain death.

When the child was born, his grandfathers rejoiced. From the auspicious placement of the planets, they could tell this boy would be a powerful ruler, just like the great King Pandu. Yudhisthira arranged festivities to celebrate the birth of his heir. He invited great sages and brahmins to perform the birth rites and gave them abundant charity.

(12:15-31) Pleased by Yudhisthira's generosity, the brahmins said, "O best of men, though your dynasty was devastated by the influence of all-powerful Time, the Supreme Lord has personally saved this boy. Because the Lord protected him, he will become famous as Vishnurata. Most fortunate one, there is no doubt that this child will become a first-class devotee decorated with all good qualities."

Yudhisthira anxiously enquired, "Will he be as powerful and virtuous as our famed ancestors?"

The chief priest, after examining the child's horoscope, said, "This boy will resemble King Ikshvaku in his ability to protect the citizens. He will be exactly like Lord Rama in taking guidance from the brahmins and in truthfulness. Comparable to the famous King Shibi in giving charity, he will protect whoever seeks his shelter and will expand your dynasty's influence as did Bharata, the son of Dushyanta. He will be a great archer like his grandfather, Arjuna. Indeed, no one will be able to defeat him.

"His physical strength will be no less than a lion's, and in his ability to shelter others, he will be like the Himalayas. He will be forgiving like the earth itself, and as tolerant as a loving parent. Like you, Yudhisthira, he will be equal toward all. He will be as liberal as Shiva and will resemble Narayana in his willingness to give protection to all supplicants. Because he always worships Krishna, he will develop qualities almost on an equal level with the Lord. In generosity he will be like the famous Rantideva, and in adherence to religious principles he will be like King Yayati. This child will grow up to be as perseverant as Bali, mighty leader of the Asuras, and in his devotion to Krishna he will equal the great Prahlada. Rest assured he will perform many sacrifices and be guided by wise and respected elders. To maintain world peace and uphold religious principles, he will be bold in punishing unruly men."

The brahmin paused and looked away, hesitating to say more. Yudhisthira became worried.

"Please do not hide anything from me," he said. "Will he face any difficulty?"

The elderly priest took a deep breath and answered, "O king, a brahmin will curse him to die by a snakebird's bite."

Yudhisthira and his four brothers looked shocked. How could such a noble king incur a brahmin's curse? They looked quizzically at the priest who explained, "This brahmin will be an immature child acting rashly. However, your grandson will take the curse as an opportunity to detach himself from the world and surrender to Krishna."

Yudhisthira felt reassured. Anything that led to Krishna's service was always auspicious. "Can you tell us more?" he asked.

The priest replied, "At that time, he will make spiritual enquiry from Shukadeva Goswami, Vyasadeva's exalted son. He will thus become purified of all material attachment and attain complete fearlessness."

Yudhisthira and his brothers gazed down affectionately at the sleeping baby. This child was surely blessed! Glad at heart, they distributed copious gifts to the brahmins.

The young prince flourished under the loving care of his five grandfathers. Whenever he would see someone for the first time, he would intently examine his face, wondering if that individual might be that same person who had rescued him while in his mother's womb.

***

(12:32-36) Shaunaka asked how Yudhisthira had funded his sacrifices so soon after a war which had exhausted his treasury. Suta explained that Krishna had told him where the ancient King Marutta had left vast gold reserves in the Himalayas. With Krishna's encouragement, Yudhisthira's brothers journeyed to the north and collected that hidden treasure, which was more than sufficient to finance three sacrifices.

Suta said, "The Pandavas were so dear to Krishna that he returned to Hastinapura to personally oversee the sacrifices, making sure that all the priests were properly qualified. He again remained for a few months with his aunt and cousins before returning to Dvaraka, accompanied by the Yadus and his intimate friend, Arjuna."

"Yudhisthira became the emperor after so much difficulty, and on Krishna's behest," said Shaunaka. "Why and when did he retire, allowing Parikit to take his place?"

Suta thanked Shaunaka for his question. "You are giving me more and more opportunities to speak about Krishna's pure devotees. This is even more powerful than speaking about the Lord himself."

Suta began to describe the incidents leading up to the Pandavas' retiring, beginning with the return to Hastinapura of the Pandavas' uncle, Vidura.

13
Vidura Instructs the Blind King

The Pandavas' beloved uncle, Vidura, returns to Hastinapura and convinces his brother Dhritarastra to retire to the forest to prepare for death. Yudhisthira is devastated when he finds Dhritarastra, his wife Gandhari, and Vidura gone. He is placated by Sage Narada's deep philosophical instructions.

(13:1-2) With mixed feelings, Vidura left Maitreya Muni. For many days, he had enjoyed hearing the great sage speak transcendental knowledge. Now, his mind was fixed on returning to Hastinapura, his birth city. When he left over thirty years earlier, he had not thought he would ever return. It was only his affection for his elder brother, Dhritarastra, that drew him back again. News reached him that Dhritarastra was still languishing in his palace, despite his advancing age and ailing health. Vidura was determined to rescue him from his attachment to material comfort and urge

103

him to take to the spiritual path. He thus set off toward the south, on the long journey to his ancestral home.

***

(13:3-6) The royal ladies gathered on the palace veranda, peering down at the unkempt mystic who strode toward the palace entrance. Kripi had seen him first, as the guards stopped him. She was intrigued when they bowed in respect to the bearded ascetic and stood aside to let him enter the palace grounds. She called Uttara and Draupadi over. "Do either of you recognise this sage?"

"Oh, Krishna!" cried out Draupadi, staring intently at the mystic as he went through the palace gates. "It looks like Uncle Vidura."

Hearing Vidura's name, Kunti ran over and looked through the window. She cried out in delight, "Vidura!"

The joyful ladies hurried to the court, sure that Vidura would go there to greet Yudhisthira. Draupadi assisted the elderly Gandhari, and Uttara held Kunti's arm. Entering the royal court, they saw Yudhisthira and the other Pandavas speaking with Dhritarastra, Kripacharya and Satyaki. The blind Dhritarastra was attended by his ever-loyal servant, Sanjaya.

As the ladies bustled in, Yudhisthira stood up in concern. "Is something wrong?"

Kunti called out, "Vidura is here!"

The men jumped up from their seats in excitement. They rushed toward the palace entrance where they saw a bedraggled but effulgent sage exchanging laughing words with a court brahmin. Immediately recognising the voice, Yudhisthira ran over and fell at the ascetic's feet.

"Uncle Vidura!" he cried. "You have returned. We thought we would never see you again."

Vidura reached down and lifted Yudhisthira to his feet. He too wept as he spoke. "Dear nephew, how I have missed you and your brothers."

Hearing Vidura's voice, Dhritarastra ran forward to greet him, with Sanjay struggling to prevent his blind master from colliding with the ornate pillars.

"My brother! You are back!" Dhritarastra cried out, his voice breaking in tearful joy.

On hearing Dhritarastra's call, Vidura turned to see him approaching with outstretched arms. The two brothers embraced one another as everyone laughed and cried in delight. Dhritarastra held his brother fast to his chest for some time, saying in a choked voice, "I feel my very life has returned to me."

Others echoed the same sentiment as Vidura greeted each of them individually. As Gandhari and Kunti were wives of his elder brothers he respectfully touched their feet in greeting. Everyone asked him questions, and he assured them that he would in time answer. Gradually they calmed down.

Yudhisthira turned to a palace attendant. "Make ready my uncle's quarters. Have the cooks prepare refreshments."

As the attendant hurried away, the Pandavas and other members of the royal court accompanied Vidura inside. They observed the Vedic rituals for receiving a respectable guest, concluding with Yudhisthira washing Vidura's feet.

(13:7-8) The next morning Vidura was given a seat of honour in the royal court. Noticing that Dhritarastra was not present, Vidura asked after him.

"Our uncle is still resting. I think the excitement of your arrival yesterday has tired him," replied Yudhisthira.

All eyes were on Vidura as Yudhisthira spoke. "My uncle, do you remember how you protected us and our mother from so many calamities? Your partiality, like the wings of a bird shielding its young, saved us from poisoning and arson."

Tears pricked Vidura's eyes. He remembered well how Duryodhana and his maternal uncle, Shakuni, had repeatedly tried to kill the young orphaned brothers. Thankfully, Vidura's spies had always alerted him to their schemes, which he had expertly foiled without bringing the hostility into the open.

(13:9-11) Yudhisthira continued. "Uncle, you have been travelling for many years. Please tell us which pilgrimage sites you visited, and how you maintained yourself. Devotees of your calibre are actually holy places incarnate since the Lord resides in your heart. Thus, you purify even sacred places with your presence."

Vidura smiled and looked down. He was not worthy of such praise, but Yudhisthira spoke out of love so he would not object. Ultimately, all abilities and opulence come from Krishna, so all praise is due to him alone.

Yudhisthira enquired about Krishna and the other Yadus. "I am sure you must have visited Dvaraka. Please give us news of our relatives, the fortunate Yadus who are always absorbed in Krishna's service. Are they happy and well?"

(13:12-16) Vidura began describing his adventures, captivating his audience with his expertise as a storyteller. However, he tactfully avoided telling them that the Yadus had all killed each other in a fierce fratricidal quarrel, and that Krishna had also departed from this world. The compassionate Vidura did not want to break this terrible news, knowing how much pain it would cause them. They would find out in due course. His mission in returning was simply to inspire Dhritarastra to give up palace life and pursue spiritual realization.

After recounting his adventures for several hours, a servant announced lunch was ready. Vidura excused himself. "I would like to spend some time with my brother. Please allow me to take my meal in his private quarters. We can speak more later."

Before departing, Vidura praised Yudhisthira's righteous rule. "As I came into your kingdom, I observed its uncommon opulence. Indeed, it resembles the very heavens, and the joyful citizens are like celestials. You and your brothers are all expert administrators, without doubt."

***

When Vidura entered his brother's private quarters, Dhritarastra and his wife Gandhari had already begun their lunch. The table was laden with a variety of choice foods cooked in ghee. Dhritarastra was complaining to his wife, "My ankles are terribly swollen, and I was again unable to sleep last night because my skin itches."

Gandhari sighed. "The doctor warned you these rich foods put too much strain on your liver. Dear husband, I implore you to follow his advice."

The old queen had taken to severe asceticism for some years and ate very little, but despite her entreaties, her husband had not followed suit. Hearing her once more suggest that he control his eating, Dhritarastra became sullen and did not reply.

Gandhari shook her head. "What can be done? You refuse to eat a simple diet and complain when you suffer the consequences."

Realising that his brother and sister-in-law had not heard him enter, Vidura said, "Have I come at a bad time?"

Startled, Dhritarastra dropped his spoon and turned his head fearfully. When he understood it was Vidura, he became jolly, remembering the many meals they had taken together. "Sit! Sit! I hoped you would come. Here are your favourite dishes."

Vidura laughed. "Brother, for over thirty years I have eaten simply. My digestion is no longer accustomed to such rich food. I will just take a little fruit."

Dhritarastra waved a hand and a servant quickly brought a large platter of fruits, from which Vidura ate a small amount. He loved his brother and it saddened him to see him still attached to material comforts. Human life was meant for realising the self, and thereby conquering the fear of death which always afflicts those overly attached to sensual pleasure.

"Yes, you have been gone for many years," said Dhritarastra. "That is the difference between us. You ran away from the world, but I cannot abandon my responsibilities. I guide Yudhisthira in all areas of policy. He would be lost without me."

He began to cough uncontrollably and spat out phlegm mixed with blood. Grasping his chest, he cried out, "Gandhari! Gandhari! Help me! I feel I am about to die! Please call the doctor immediately!"

The elderly blind-folded Gandhari fumbled her way to her husband's side. Commanding the maid to call the doctor, she frantically rubbed Dhritarastra's back and chest. Soon, the doctor rushed in to find him perspiring heavily. Vidura sat silently as the doctor massaged Dhritarastra's chest, gave him medicines, and chided him for continuing to eat such rich food. When he left, Dhritarastra lay down, exhausted from his ordeal. Gandhari sat at her husband's feet and gently pressed his legs.

"It's my heart!" Dhritarastra told Vidura by way of explanation. "Often I cannot sleep because of the severe pains in my chest. I think it is stress. Bhima is so vicious and unforgiving. He stands outside my window and loudly boasts of the day he broke Duryodhana's thigh in battle. Other times he jokes about how he ripped out Dushashana's heart and drank his blood. I think if it were not for Yudhisthira, that vengeful man would also tear out my heart."

(13:17) As he spoke, Dhritarastra became increasingly agitated. Vidura shook his head. His blind brother was so attached to family affairs he could not see how time was stealing away his life.

(13:18-20) Vidura took his brother's hands into his own. "My dear king, please leave this place immediately with me. Just see how fear has overtaken you. If we remain in the bodily concept of life, the Lord in the form of Time will snatch from us all we possess, including our very life; what to speak of our wealth, honour, children, land and home."

Dhritarastra pulled his hands away. "What are you saying, Brother? Where should I go? I am not like you. I am accustomed to palace life. I cannot live as a mendicant."

(13:21-22) Vidura went on, "Your father, brother, well-wishers and sons are all dead and gone. Your life is all but over, your body is overtaken by invalidity and you are living in the home of another. You have been blind from your very birth, and now your hearing is failing. Your memory is shortened, and your intelligence is disturbed. Your teeth are loose, your liver is defective, and you are coughing up mucous."

Dhritarastra winced. "Do not speak so harshly, Vidura. Remember, I am your elder brother."

(13:23) Vidura stood and walked up and down the room in exasperation. "Alas!" he cried. "How powerful are the hopes of a living being to continue his life. Verily, you are living just like a household dog, eating remnants of food given by Bhima."

"That's not true!" exclaimed Dhritarastra, turning away from Vidura, finding the accusation too difficult to swallow.

(13:24) Vidura sat next to his brother and placed a hand upon his shoulder. "Dear brother, there is no need to live a degraded life and subsist on the charity of those whom you tried to kill by arson and poisoning."

Dhritarastra's mouth fell open. No one had referred to those incidents for many years. He had blocked them from his mind.

"Do not look so surprised, Brother," said Vidura. "Yudhisthira may treat you like his chief counsellor, but I know he has not forgotten your mistreatment of him. How could he? After all, you grievously insulted Draupadi and usurped their kingdom and wealth."

Dhritarastra winced. "Have you returned to simply cause me pain?"

(13:25) In despair, Vidura stood up and exclaimed, "Despite your unwillingness to die and your desire to live even at the cost of honour and prestige, your miserly body will certainly dwindle and deteriorate like an old garment."

(13:26-27) Kneeling next to Dhritarastra's bed, Vidura's voice became pleading. "Brother, listen to me. In old age, a wise person goes to an unknown, remote place and, freed of attachment, quits his material body when it has become useless. Such a first-class man realises the falsity and misery of this material world. He thus leaves home to depend fully on the Lord dwelling within his heart."

Dhritarastra sighed. His brother was always given to speaking unpalatable truths. No matter how hard they were to hear, time had proven their value again and again. In the past, to his great detriment, he had ignored his brother's pleas. Yet still Vidura had returned to help him. Relinquishing his pride, Dhritarastra sat up in his bed and said, "You speak the truth, Brother, but what can I do?"

(13:28-30) Vidura shed tears of relief. "My dear brother, please leave with me this very night. We shall go toward the north. Do not let anyone know."

"I must tell Yudhisthira," objected Dhritarastra.

"No, Brother," insisted Vidura. "He will try to convince you to stay here."

Dhritarastra hesitated. "Maybe I should stay. After all, I am blind."

Vidura spoke urgently. "You must try to become detached from material life, otherwise, you will be forced to take birth again."

"I have performed many sacrifices in this life. I will surely get a good rebirth."

"You do not understand," said Vidura. "Kali Yuga is approaching. All good qualities of men will greatly diminish. Better to get out of this material world in this life rather than risk another birth in the terrible Kali age."

He placed a reassuring hand on Dhritarastra's arm and added, "I will help you, Brother. I will guide you every step of the way."

Dhritarastra sat in thought. He knew that to be guided by a saint like Vidura was a rare and invaluable opportunity. He also knew about Kali Yuga. Vidura was right. Now was the time to become serious about spiritual salvation. He replied softly, "Very well, let us go!"

Gandhari broke her silence, and rising said, "Dear husband, I have been ever faithful and obedient to you. Pray, therefore, take me with you. I, too, wish to cut my attachment to material existence."

Dhritarastra and Vidura both agreed, confident of Gandhari's capacity for austerity. Taking nothing, they left secretly soon after sunset.

(13:31) The next morning, as was his custom, Yudhisthira rose before dawn and performed his worship of the Lord. He was joined by learned brahmins who gave him scriptural instructions. As they left, he respectfully offered them grains, cows, land and money in charity. Then, as usual, he went to pay his respects to his elderly uncle and aunt, Dhritarastra and Gandhari, thinking he would find Vidura with them.

Approaching their quarters, he saw Sanjay slumped on the floor, weeping.

"My dear Sanjay, what is wrong?" Yudhisthira asked.

(13:32) Sanjay looked up, his eyes reddened from crying. Turning toward Dhritarastra's inner chambers, he shook his head sadly. Filled with a sense of foreboding, Yudhisthira entered his uncle's residence, but there was no sign of him or Gandhari. Vidura was also missing. Walking briskly through their quarters, he called their names, but there was no reply. This was most unusual. Returning to Sanjay, Yudhisthira anxiously questioned him. "Where are my uncles and aunt, Sanjay?"

(13:33) Dhritarastra's servant kept his head down, weeping uncontrollably. Yudhisthira's anxiety increased. "Has the grief of their sons' death finally overcome them? Have they, pained by my grievous offenses toward them, drowned themselves in the Ganges?"

(13:34) Feelings of guilt and separation overwhelmed Yudhisthira and he lamented piteously. "When we were young orphans, Dhritarastra and Vidura took us in and protected us. Please tell me what has happened to them?"

(13:35-37) At first, Sanjay was unable to reply but simply sobbed. Gradually, he calmed himself, and wiping away his tears replied in a strained voice, "My dear descendant of the Kuru dynasty, I have no idea where they went. O king, they have cheated me, for although I have been Dhritarastra's ever-faithful servant, he left me without a word."

(13:38) News reached Narada of the Pandavas' apprehension for their elderly uncles and aunt and he decided to visit Hastinapura. When the sage arrived, playing his lute, Yudhisthira and his brothers rose from their seats to welcome him. After the formal reception was complete and they were all seated, Narada enquired about the welfare of the Pandavas' family.

(13:39-40) Yudhisthira sighed. "O godly personality, I do not know where my two uncles have gone. Nor can I find my ascetic aunt who is devastated by the loss of all her sons. Please guide us. You are like the captain of a ship that take us across this ocean of grief."

(13:41-43) Narada replied, "O king, do not lament for anyone, for everyone is under the Lord's control."

To assure Yudhisthira that his uncles and aunt had not left for any fault of his, Narada explained that all living beings are bound by their God-given duties, as a cow is bound by a long rope.

"My dear Yudhisthira," Narada said, "it is the duty of royalty to renounce the world at the end of life in order to pursue spiritual enlightenment. Their departure is, therefore, desired by Krishna. As a player sets up and disperses his playthings according to his own sweet will, so the supreme will of the Lord brings men together and separates them."

(13:44) Still Yudhisthira's grief could not be assuaged. He held his head in his hands and wept, thinking of the dangers his blind elders faced. Narada lovingly chided him. "My dear king, your grief is due to illusory affection and nothing more."

Yudhisthira looked up, confusion evident in his eyes. Was he meant to have no feeling for his elders?

Narada continued, "Consider this, Yudhisthira, if a person is the body, then your affection is for its chemical constituents. Is that sensible? If the person is a spirit soul, then why lament? The soul continues unharmed, even with the body's demise. If the soul is a manifestation of the all-pervasive spirit, at the time of death he returns to that spirit. If you say the person is both the soul and the body, then still there is no reason for lamentation as the elements comprising the body continue to exist, as does the soul.

(13:45) "Therefore your agitation is due only to ignorance. Stop foolishly thinking that without your protection they will suffer. The Lord alone protects us. We must simply do our duty."

Yudhisthira's body relaxed. Narada's words made sense. Still, it was hard to give up his sense of responsibility for his ailing elders.

(13:46) Seeing the king's lingering unhappiness, Narada patiently continued to instruct him.

"Everyone's material body is under the influence of nature, time, and their karmic reactions. People in the modes of ignorance and passion are unable to help anyone for they cannot see things as they are. Those in goodness can help others to some extent. Even then, by the influence of time and destiny they will eventually be frustrated. Time is like a cobra whose bite is always lethal. How can a person who is himself under time's influence help others?"

(13:47) Yudhisthira remained morose. His uncle and aunt were accustomed to being served the finest foods. How would they survive in the jungle? Narada reminded him that everyone depends on Krishna for food. By his arrangement one living being was food for another. In the forest there were wild fruits and vegetables which could sustain a person.

Wiping away his tears, Yudhisthira said, "If we are all controlled by nature, time and karma, in what sense do we depend on Krishna?"

(13:48) "This is a good question," replied Narada. "Try to understand everything is the Lord's energy, including the living entities, the modes of nature, time and karma. As such, it is all under his supreme control. Only because we forget this, do we suffer. Therefore, the Lord manifests within us as the Supersoul, and without, as the spiritual master and scripture, just to rectify our errant mentality. Only by taking his guidance can we remain undisturbed by material happiness and distress.

(1:49-50) Placing a reassuring hand on Yudhisthira's arm, Narada said, "Time is merely another form of your friend, Krishna. As Time, he destroys the faithless, but he is not at all dangerous to his faithful devotees. He came to the earth to help the gods by annihilating the miscreants. Soon he will end his earthly pastimes. When Krishna departs, good king, you and your brothers should also leave.

(13:51-53) "As for your uncle and aunt; along with Vidura they have gone to the southern side of the Himalayas, to the Shaptashrota region, where the sages reside. Dhritarastra has begun the practise of mystic yoga, bathing thrice daily and taking only water. He will thus become free of familial attachment.

(13:54-58) By the breathing process he will turn his senses toward Brahman and rise above the influence of material nature. By ceasing all sensual activity, he will become fixed in trance. Merging with the Supreme, he will then rise to the spiritual sky. Most probably on the fifth day from now he will quit his body in the fire of self-immolation, which will burn his thatched cottage to ashes. His chaste wife will enter that fire with fixed mind and go with him to the eternal atmosphere."

"What about Vidura?" asked Yudhisthira

(13:59-60) "Afflicted with delight and grief, he will leave that sacred place and continue his pilgrimage."

The sage then took his leave and ascended into space. Yudhisthira sat in thought. He felt relieved of his concern for Dhritarastra and Gandhari, but Narada's words had filled him with another anxiety. Krishna's departure was imminent. Would it be possible to see him again before that time? He asked Arjuna to go immediately to Dvaraka to ask the Lord about his plans.

14. Ominous Portents

Arjuna is away far longer than expected. Yudhisthira observes inauspicious omens and is worried that Krishna may have already departed. When Arjuna returns, he is very distressed.

(14:1-21) Months passed and Arjuna did not return. Yudhisthira began to observe fearful omens. Blood rained down with dust storms and cloudless thunder. Crows shrieked and jackals bayed. The people were quarrelsome, and the deities in temples appeared as if crying and about to leave.

Yudhisthira anxiously conferred with Bhima. "It is seven months since Arjuna left. See now these terrible portents. Has the time for the Lord's departure arrived, as Narada indicated? How can we live without him? All our success came from him. He is our only support. These fearful signs indicate the Earth's good fortune has ended, for the Lord will no longer place upon her his lotus-like feet."

(14:22-44) The king continued to fret until at last Arjuna returned. Seeing him entering the royal court, Yudhisthira jumped down from his throne and hurried toward him. Arjuna appeared downcast, and he sighed repeatedly. Yudhisthira clasped both his brother's hands in his own. For some moments, he gazed at Arjuna, who looked down at the floor, constantly shedding tears. Remembering the fateful words of Narada, Yudhisthira began to question him with great apprehension.

"Tell me, dear brother, are the Yadus and their friends well? Is my respectable grandfather, Surasena, happy? Are Uncle Vasudeva, his brothers and his wives all in good spirits? Are Ugrasena, Akrura, Hridika, Jayanta, Gada, Sarana and Satrujit all faring well? How is Balarama, the Supreme Lord and protector of the devotees?"

Continuously weeping, Arjuna made no reply. Yudhisthira wrung his hands in anxiety. Had Krishna ended his pastimes? He went on naming the residents of Dvaraka, including Krishna himself, asking after their welfare.

"The great Yadu heroes, protected by the Lord's powerful arms, enjoy life like the residents of Vaikuntha. Krishna's loving wives enjoy opulence and pleasures meant for the king of heaven. All his relatives are fearless in every respect and their feet trample over the celestial Sudharma assembly house, which they took from the gods. Pray tell me, Arjuna, how are they now?"

As Yudhisthira pressed Arjuna for news of the Yadus, the colour drained from Arjuna's face. His body trembled and tears streamed from his eyes. Yudhisthira anxiously asked, "My dear Arjuna, is your health good? What has disturbed you? Is it due to others disrespecting you because of your long stay at Dvaraka? Has someone addressed you with unfriendly words or threatened you? Could you not give charity to one who asked, or could you not keep your promise to someone?"

The king placed his bejeweled hands on his brother's shoulders. "You always protected deserving living beings, such as brahmins, children, cows, women and the disabled. Could you not safeguard them when they asked you for shelter? Have you mistreated a woman? Or have you been defeated on the way by someone inferior or equal to you?"

Yudhisthira sighed deeply. Surely his suspicions about Krishna were true. Arjuna could not be guilty of any of his speculative suggestions. In a voice thick with anxiety and sorrow he said, "Or could it be that you are feeling empty for all time, due to losing your most intimate friend, Krishna? Dear brother, I can think of no other reason for your despondency."

15. The Pandavas Depart

After hearing that Krishna and his family have all left this world, the Pandavas decide to retire.

(15:1-5) For some moments, Arjuna said nothing. Remembering the Lord's kindness, friendship, intimate familial relations and his chariot driving, Arjuna was overwhelmed with feelings of separation. Composing himself with great effort, he began to speak.

"The Supreme Lord, Krishna, who treated me as his dearest friend, has left me. I have just lost he whose absence for a moment would render all the worlds repulsive, like bodies without life. Because of his departure, my astounding power, that amazed even the gods, is also gone."

Arjuna again broke down weeping. Yudhisthira gaped at him, unable to speak. His other brothers had entered the court on hearing of Arjuna's return. They, too, looked shocked. Krishna had left?! Their greatest well-wishing friend and beloved Lord. Weakened by the news, they stumbled to their seats, burying their faces in their hands.

(15:6-31) Once seated, Arjuna collected his thoughts and calmed himself. Taking a deep breath, he said, "By Krishna's grace, I overcame the world's monarchs to win the celestially beautiful Draupadi, succeeding in a near-impossible test of arms. With him by my side, I defeated the gods in a battle and compelled the celestial architect Mayadanava to build the incomparable Mayasabha assembly house. And thanks to him, our brother, Bhima, was able to slay King Jarasandha, who had conquered thousands of other kings."

Arjuna's brothers listened in stunned silence as he recalled the numerous times Krishna had saved them from catastrophe; particularly during the Battle of Kurukshetra.

"The Kauravas' military strength was like an ocean in which dwelt many invincible shark-like fighters. It was insurmountable. Only because of Krishna's friendship was I able to cross it safely. By his mere glance, he withdrew those warriors' life duration. The Lord thus sapped the inspiration, power and enthusiasm from the prodigious martial array headed by Bhishma, Karna, Drona, Shalya, and other mighty heroes. Their arrangement was expert and insuperable, but Krishna neutralised it as he drove my chariot forward. The great generals, although directing unstoppable weapons at me, could not touch even a hair on my head."

As he remembered his familiarity with Krishna, Arjuna trembled with grief. "Surely it was only due to a lack of esteem for my Lord that I dared engage him as my chariot driver, for he is worshiped and offered services by the best of men who desire salvation. Krishna and I would eat, sleep and pass our leisure hours together. I became so intimate with him that I would joke and playfully deride him, laughing

121

when he spoke of his chivalry, saying, 'Of course, my friend, of course!' He never took offence and excused my audacity exactly as a friend would excuse another friend, or a lover, his beloved. Separated from my dearest well-wisher, the best of all persons, my heart is broken and there is no purpose to my life."

The five brothers sat in stunned silence for some time, thinking only of Krishna. Their grief from Krishna's separation intensified their loving feelings and they forgot everything else, even the existence of their own bodies.

Arjuna became increasingly disconsolate as he explained how after Krishna's departure, he had been entrusted to bring the Lord's queens to Hastinapura. "I was then attacked by a band of ruffian cowherds who kidnapped those ladies despite my attempts to protect them. I fought with the same Gandiva bow, with which I overcame the gods. I rode upon the same chariot, carried the same inexhaustible quiver of arrows, and I am the same Arjuna who was respected and feared by all. Yet, in an instant, it has all been rendered useless due to Krishna's absence."

Arjuna's brothers looked at him in disbelief. Defeated by cowherd men?!

Arjuna told Yudhisthira of the fate of Krishna's family and dynasty. "Since you asked me about the Yadus, I will tell you, though it pains me greatly. Intoxicated with wine and afflicted by a brahminical curse, they fought together with iron bars, hardly recognising each other. Now all but four or five of them are dead and gone."

His four brothers turned ashen. How could the virtuous Yadus have killed one another? It was unthinkable. Bhima was the first to speak. "Surely this was engineered by Krishna so that his associates would leave with him. How else could the Lord's invincible sons and grandsons have been slain? No one on earth could have killed them."

Arjuna agreed it had been Krishna's will. "As in the ocean the bigger fish swallow the smaller, so the Lord engaged one Yadu to kill another, and then he, too, departed."

Becoming silent, Arjuna began to meditate on the instructions Krishna had spoken at the commencement of the Battle of Kurukshetra.[30] Gradually, he felt his sorrow subside and his mind become free from illusion.

(15:32-50) Yudhisthira began to think of the future. He knew that in Krishna's absence, Kali's influence would spread, characterized by increasing avarice, falsehood, cheating and violence. He remembered that Narada had instructed him to retire and follow his Lord. Thus he made arrangements for Parikit to be crowned as the next king of Hastinapura. He also installed Krishna's great grandson, Vajra, as the king in Mathura.

After enthroning Parikit and Vajra, he and his brothers gave up their royal dress and put on simple cloth. With their minds fixed on attaining Krishna's eternal association, they set out from their city without telling anyone. They walked toward the mountains, oblivious to everything, and appearing like madmen. In due course, they left this world and went to Krishna's eternal spiritual planet. Their wife, Draupadi, and mother, Kunti, also fixed their minds on the Lord and ascended to his abode.

***

(15:34-35) As Suta brought his narrative to an end, the sages sat in silence, many of them shedding tears. Krishna and his entire family, as well as the mighty Pandavas and their relatives, were all gone. What a terrible loss for the earth. How unfortunate they were not to have been able to see them.

Sensing their mood, Suta spoke. "The Lord and his pastimes are eternal, always visible to his pure devotees. Please also understand the Yadus did not die in the same way a conditioned soul dies. Many of the gods entered the Yadu family to assist the Lord in killing the demonic kings. On the pretext of a fratricidal slaughter, those gods returned to their heavenly posts. The Lord's eternal associates, however, returned with him to his never-ending pastimes in the eternal Dvaraka. The Pandavas also reached him in their self-same spiritual bodies, in which they always serve him."

Shaunaka sat quietly, assimilating this information. It was not easy to understand Krishna's activities. After some moments he said, "Did Krishna take part in the fight between the Yadus? Did he, like them, also leave his body?"

Suta said, "Krishna never gives up his body. All his forms are eternal, sometimes manifest and sometimes not. Like a magician, he seems to relinquish his body, but he never factually has a material form."

"Will his apparent death not confuse people into thinking he is like them?" asked Shaunaka.

"The devotees are never confused," replied Suta. "Only the atheists will take this episode as proof that Krishna is a mere mortal. This is Krishna's desire, for he never reveals himself to those who envy him. Thus, he creates an illusion of his departure."

"It is not a happy illusion," stated Shaunaka, smiling weakly.

(15:51) Suta chuckled. "No my friend; but grief for the departure of the Lord and his great devotees is another aspect of *prema*. Indeed, anyone who faithfully hears such subjects will attain pure devotion to Krishna."

Loud shouts of approval arose from the sages. Shaunaka said, "Pray tell us what happened after the Pandavas left and Parikit assumed the throne."

16. Parikit Becomes King

Parikit sees signs of Kali Yuga's degradation appearing in the world and sets out on an expedition to purge the earth of all corrupt elements. Meanwhile, the earth goddess, Bhumi, and the god of religion, Dharma, come to the earth and speak together about their harassed condition.

(16:1-9) Suta began to narrate Parikit's history.

"Parikit perfectly fulfilled all the predictions made by the brahmins at his birth. Under his reign, the world prospered. With the elderly Kripacharya as his chief priest, he performed great religious rituals at which even ordinary men saw the gods. After marrying Princess Iravati of Virata, he fathered four sons who became powerful rulers of the earth."

Suta described how Parikit encountered the personality of Kali who presides over the age. "Finding Kali attacking a cow and bull, the king arrested him."

(16:5-8) "Why did he not just kill him?" asked Shaunaka. "Surely that is the appropriate punishment for such a crime. Besides which, how did he ascertain that it was Kali?"

As soon as he asked the question, Shaunaka had second thoughts. He did not want to distract Suta from speaking about Krishna.

"Dear Suta, my enquiry was foolish. No one here is interested in worldly politics. We only want to hear discussions about Krishna, which are like the nectar of immortality. Any other subjects merely steal away one's duration of life. Indeed, the very lord of death, Yamaraja himself, is attracted to hear about Krishna. Therefore, those who always engage in such discussions will not fall victim to his influence."

(16:9) Looking over the assembly of sages, many of whom were nodding in concurrence with his words, Shaunaka concluded, "We do not want to be like foolish men who waste their short lives uselessly engaged either in idle talks and works, or in sleeping; thus never finding time to hear about Krishna."

Suta reassured Shaunaka that because the question related to the actions of the great devotee, Parikit, the answer was as enlightening as topics directly dealing with Krishna. "Indeed, histories of the Lord's great devotees are as spiritually powerful as those about Krishna himself. I shall therefore answer your question by describing this episode. Please listen."

***

(16:10-24) Parikit sat on his throne, deep in thought. He had just returned from an incognito tour of his kingdom, and was greatly disturbed by what he had seen. Moving about the country in disguise, he found his citizens engaging in sinful activities. He saw some drinking liquor, others gambling and still others engaging in public displays of passion. How was this possible under his rule? News had previously reached him of neighbouring states that were straying from the path of *dharma* under the rule of impious kings. It seemed their influence was infiltrating his own kingdom.

Determining to rectify the situation, the king commanded his minister, "Ready the troops. We shall march tomorrow at dawn."

Although the degradation in his domain was troubling, as a mighty warrior, Parikit was pleased for an opportunity to exercise his military prowess. He embarked at once on an expedition to ensure all parts of the globe were cleansed of corruption. Mounting a war-chariot drawn by great black steeds and bearing the emblem of a lion, he rode out at the head of a vast army. Wherever he traveled, he heard stirring recitations of his forefathers' glories, especially of the Pandavas and their intimate relationship with Krishna. He heard how the Lord had protected and even served them. Listening to these accounts, Parikit's eyes welled with tears of ecstasy. He rewarded the speakers with priceless pearl necklaces and costly garments.

Parikit asserted his righteous rule throughout the earth, including those regions, inhabited by celestial beings, which ordinarily cannot be reached by humans. As he continued on his campaign, the earth goddess, Bhumi, and religion personified, Dharma, came to the world. Appearing as a cow and a bull respectively, they met together. Bhumi wept piteously as Dharma questioned her.

"Good lady, why do you appear so sad? Are you lamenting because in this terrible age low class men will exploit your resources, wantonly slaughtering poor animals? Or are you distressed because the gods will stop receiving your produce in sacrificial offerings? Perhaps you are sorry because soon the creatures you sustain will have to endure famine and drought. Is your anguish due to the impending proliferation of irreligious brahmin*s* and atheistic, corrupt leaders who will abuse women and children? Or are you sorry because the general populace will soon abandon the rules of civilised life?"

Dharma concluded that the greatest misfortune was the termination of Krishna's earthly pastimes. "This must be why you are now feeling bereft. Time is surely invincible, for I see that even you, the reservoir of riches, have been reduced to this pitiable state."

(16:25-36) With her large and doleful eyes, Bhumi looked at Dharma in his form as a pure white bull and said, "Great lord of religion, I see that you, too, are in a sorry condition. Once, you stood firmly on your four legs, increasing happiness all over the universe."

Bhumi shed tears to see Dharma's pitiful condition. His four legs were truth, austerity, mercy and cleanliness, the four chief principles of religion. With each successive age, one of them had been broken. Now that the age of Kali had arrived, he stood on only the leg of truth. Even that was now threatened.

Taking a deep breath, Bhumi continued, "Oh, where has the Lord gone? All goodness resides in him and in his presence we flourished. While the Lord's auspicious footprints graced me, I felt unlimitedly blessed. Previously, I had been distressed because I was overburdened by the military forces of ambitious demons. You also suffered at the hands of these atheists and we were relieved only by Krishna's merciful appearance. Now, in his absence, Kali spreads his evil everywhere."

17. Parikit Arrests Kali

Parikit encounters Bhumi and Dharma as they are being assailed by Kali, whom he subdues. Beseeched by Kali, the king spares him but restricts the areas where he may reside.

(17:1-20) Soon after Dharma and Bhumi's conversation, Parikit entered that region. From a distance, he saw a man of blackish complexion, dressed like a king, beating the celestial cow and bull with a stick. As he came closer, he saw the bull was terrified and the cow was crying.

Parikit at once drew his sword and shouted, "Stop, you wretch! You dress like a king, but you act like the lowest of men. How dare you impersonate the royal order and assail helpless creatures under my care? Do you think because Krishna and Arjuna are gone, you can indulge freely in such sin? I am here to check you. Death is the fitting punishment for this vile act."

The assailant shrank back from Parikit, who raised his great sword in readiness to cut him down. Keeping the man in check, Parikit tried to establish how such a heinous crime had occurred in his kingdom.

Turning to the bull, he enquired, "Are you really a bull or are you a god who has come to foretell the future sufferings of cows and bulls? Never before have I seen anyone who lives under the jurisdiction of the Kuru kings grieve due to lack of a protector."

Parikit glowered at the cowering aggressor. How had he been able to commit such an outrage? It was an unimaginable transgression in a Kuru kingdom. He turned back to Dharma.

"O noble bull, give up your dejection. I will ensure your safety."

Parikit then reassured Bhumi. "Dear mother cow, as long as I rule this land there is no cause for you to cry. Everything will be auspicious for you."

Parikit assured them both their attacker would be punished. "A king's prime duty is to protect his citizens from suffering at the hands of criminals. If I fail in this duty, my reputation, prosperity, and fate in the afterlife will all be jeopardized. Therefore, I will kill this monstrous wretch because he has inflicted needless violence on you."

Addressing the bull, Parikit asked, "Who is this vile man who has caused you so much suffering? Do you know his name or where he comes from?" In the state of the kings obedient to God's laws, there is surely no one suffering as you are now. Indeed, until now, no one has shed tears as a result of royal negligence. O bull, I wish you all good. Please identify this villain, whose crimes blacken the reputation of my illustrious forefathers."

Looking toward Kali, the king's tone became menacing.

"Whoever causes innocent living beings to suffer must fear me anywhere and everywhere. Any upstart who commits offenses by torturing others shall be uprooted, even if he is a denizen of heaven with armour and decorations. The king's supreme duty is to protect law-abiding persons and chastise miscreants."

Dharma replied, "Your words surely befit a descendant of the Pandavas. Captivated by their love and devotion, Lord Krishna himself served as their messenger. What then could they not achieve?"

Parikit kept his sword raised over the cowering Kali as Dharma answered the king's question.

"O mighty hero, it is difficult to know who is to blame for my condition, for I am confused by various philosophical views. Some maintain we suffer due to our sins, while others contend that nature brings about all miseries as a matter of course. Some say the self is entirely to blame, and others say there are greater powers at work. Still others suggest it is never possible to know the cause of distress, no matter how hard we try. Please ponder it with your own intelligence, great king, and do what you think is right."

(17:21-35) Impressed by this reply, Parikit respectfully enquired, "Who are you? You cannot be an ordinary bull, as you understand the deep truths of religion. One who considers another the cause of his suffering is as much in illusion as one who inflicts suffering on others. I think you must be the personality of religion, Dharma, for no one else could be so sagacious."

After deducing the bull's true identity, Parikit could understand the significance of his three broken legs. He said, "Formerly, in the golden age of Satya, your four legs were established as the four principles of austerity, cleanliness, mercy and truthfulness. It appears that three of your legs were broken over time, due to rampant irreligion in the form of pride, lust, and intoxication. You are now standing on only the leg of truthfulness."

Parikit glared at the bull's assailant. "This must be Kali, who personifies quarrel and hypocrisy, and under whom deceit flourishes. It appears he wants to destroy truthfulness, the last leg of religion."

Parikit looked with concern at the afflicted Dharma. He knew that while Krishna had been personally present, all four of his legs had been restored, but now in the Lord's absence, religion had again deteriorated. Consequently, the earth's burden was increasing.

Inspecting the cow carefully, he realised she was Bhumi. She was crying for what awaited her, when lower-class men would pose as rulers and abuse her and her children. With great sympathy, he pacified Dharma and Bhumi, then turned toward Kali and drew back his sword.

Kali shook with fear. Quickly casting off his royal dress, he fell at Parikit's feet and begged for his life.

"Spare me. I surrender unto you."

Kali knew he had no power over a person fully devoted to Krishna. He caught hold of the king's feet in supplication. "Command me, lord. I am your servant."

Parikit lowered his sword. "I cannot kill a surrendered person, but you must leave my kingdom. If you are allowed to pose as a leader or influence other leaders, irreligion will become rampant. Greed, falsehood, robbery, incivility, treachery, misfortune, cheating, quarrel and vanity will soon abound."

(17:36-37) Kali bowed his head and spoke imploringly. "Where shall I live? Your rule extends throughout the entire world. You will hunt me down

133

wherever I go. Still, I am your subject, and therefore entitled to your protection. Pray grant me a residence."

Parikit examined the trembling Kali. His arrival had surely been by divine arrangement. Sometimes the only way a person can be rectified is by receiving the natural consequences of his foolishness. Kali's influence would doubtlessly cause iniquity amongst the people, but the painful results would eventually bring them to their senses. The king also knew the Age of Kali provided a unique opportunity for conditioned souls to return to the spiritual world simply by chanting the Lord's holy name. Only those too foolish to take to this process would fall victim to Kali's sway.

(17:38-45) Parikit said, "You may reside in those places where gambling, intoxication, prostitution and animal slaughter are found."

Kali looked dejected. Where in Parikit's kingdom—which encompassed the entire world— would he find such activities? He begged for somewhere else where he might stay. Parikit relented. "Very well, you may also live wherever gold is hoarded."

Kali thanked the king. Now he had a place to go—many places. Gold was greatly coveted throughout the world. Wherever gold was stored, it created a fertile situation for envy, enmity and other forms of sin to proliferate. Satisfied, Kali backed away from Parikit and disappeared.

When Kali had gone, Parikit carefully tended to Dharma, again restoring his four legs. The king felt confident that while he ruled, Kali would not again attack virtue. Even if he influenced the minds of the less intelligent, Parikit would ensure they would not be able to follow Kali's dictates. The powerful king vigilantly ruled the world with justice and compassion, ensuring that piety flourished.

18. Parikit Cursed

On a hunting expedition, Parikit, afflicted by thirst, uncharacteristically insults a meditating sage and is cursed to die in seven days by the sage's son.

(18:5-8) Suta Goswami said, "Thus did the intelligent King Parikit deal with Kali, who had entered the world on the very day Krishna departed. He felt no antagonism toward him because he knew the Lord had arranged special concessions in Kali's age."

Intrigued, Shaunaka asked what these were.

"In this age, one has only to think of a pious act in order to reap its benefit, but sinful acts must be performed before one gets a reaction."

"This is wonderful," agreed Shaunaka, "but sadly, people's sinful thoughts can soon become their acts."

"Indeed," replied Suta, "but there is another great advantage of Kali Yuga. Merely by hearing and chanting about Krishna, one can purify his mind and achieve complete liberation. Knowing this, King Parikit widely propagated the chanting of Krishna's name and glories. His citizens were thus protected from Kali's influence. Only those who foolishly neglect Krishna's service, need fear Kali."

Shaunaka remarked, "It is astonishing that such a great king was cursed by a brahmin! What did he do on hearing about the curse?"

(18:1-3) Suta replied, "Since Parikit had full faith in Krishna, who saved him even as an unborn child, he accepted the curse as the Lord's auspicious arrangement. Unafraid of death, he left everything, and became Sage Shukadeva's disciple. Under his guidance, the king was able to attain Krishna's association at the time of death."

Shaunaka marveled at how Parikit saw the Lord's merciful arrangement in such apparent reversal. He asked how one can cultivate such a disposition.

(18:4,9,10) Suta said, "Those who dedicate their lives to systematically hearing about Krishna, who performs wonderful acts, will always remember him. Even at death they will not fall victim to fear, which is born of ignorance."

Suta paused and looked around the assembly of attentive sages. "As you did ask me, so I have related to you the pious history of King Parikit. He perfectly demonstrates the great benefit of hearing about the Lord. Now, what more do you wish to know?"

(18:12) The sages were delighted by Suta's clear explanation. They had started the day feeling anxious because they knew their fire sacrifices were inadequate to save people from Kali Yuga. Now they felt cheerful; reassured that hearing about Krishna was the solution they sought.

(18:11) One sage called out, "O sober-minded Suta, we are indebted to you. May you live long and achieve everlasting fame, for you are describing

Krishna's activities, which are the elixir of immortality for mortals like us."

(18:13-17) Another said, "Dear Suta, the value of associating with a devotee of your calibre is inestimable. No material gains can compare; even attaining heaven or liberation. Indeed, those who seek such things only condemn themselves to repeated birth and death. The intelligent never tire of hearing discourses about Govinda, which bestow the highest benefit."

Another sage added, "We are now convinced Krishna is greater than even Brahma or Shiva. He alone protects all living beings, therefore the wise constantly hear about him."

Shaunaka requested Suta to repeat Shukadeva's instructions to Parikit, hearing which the king had attained Krishna's personal association at the time of death.

(18:18-23) Suta withdrew into himself for a few moments. Then he replied, "My dear Shaunaka, you and the sages here are godly brahmins, but I am a low-class person. Somehow or other I received the good fortune of hearing from the great Shukadeva. By his association I have been purified, and by chanting the name of the unlimitedly powerful Lord, the disqualification of my degraded birth has been destroyed. Thus, you have accepted me in your midst."

Suta paused, tears flowing down his cheeks as he thought of his spiritual master's mercy. The sages sat in respectful silence as he continued.

"How can anyone describe the glories of Krishna, who is the worshipful Lord of Shiva and Brahma? The water that washed his toenail purifies the very universe. Those attached to him can immediately give up this world to attain life's highest perfection, thereby becoming completely peaceful and renounced. It is impossible to fully delineate Krishna's glories, but as birds fly in the limitless sky to the limit of their power, so shall I do my best to repeat what I have heard."

Shaunaka entreated Suta, "Pray describe to us the circumstances culminating in Parikit's surrender to Shukadeva."

Suta agreed. "Yes, I will tell you everything about this."

**

(18:24-31) Parikit rose before sunrise as was his habit. After performing his daily worship, he left on a hunting expedition at the crack of dawn. It was a particularly hot and humid morning. By mid-morning, the king was extremely thirsty and fatigued. While searching for a reservoir of water, Parikit came upon the hermitage of the well-known sage, Shamika. The king found him seated with his eyes half-closed in meditation. The emaciated sage wore only a loincloth. He had unkempt matted hair and was sat upon a deerskin. Parikit could just make out the barely audible intonation of the sacred syllable 'Om'. Normally out of respect for the meditating sage, the king would have left at once, but today, impelled by his burning thirst, he announced his presence.

"I am King Parikit, your humble servant. I come to offer respects and to request your hospitality. Pray allow me to take a little water."

Parikit prostrated himself before the sage, who did not acknowledge his presence nor even move slightly. Rising, Parikit again addressed him.

"Great sage, there is no need for a mere king to instruct a learned brahmin like yourself. Surely you are well aware of the scriptural injunction that a guest should at least be received with sweet words, water and a place to sit. Therefore, although I am of a lower caste, I seek your hospitality."

Still the sage stayed silent. Parikit scowled and looked around the small, bare hut. There was a clay water pot in the corner, but Parikit did not want to take it without permission. He felt irritated that Shamika did not say anything; convinced the sage was feigning trance just to avoid receiving a member of a lower order of life.

Tired, thirsty and feeling insulted, he strode out of the hut. Near the entrance, he saw a dead snake. Impelled by destiny, he picked it up with the end of his bow and placed it around the sage's neck as if it were a garland. He felt this was a fitting response for the cold reception Shamika had given him.

As he rode back toward his capital, Hastinapura, he began to regret his rash act. Had the sage really been pretending? It seemed unlikely. Surely had made a grave mistake. He had foolishly insulted a saintly person even as he was engaged in his holy meditations. Parikit was struck by remorse. How had he allowed anger to overcome him? Greatly troubled in mind, the king entered his capital, where crowds of joyous people thronged the streets to greet him.

***

(18:32-50) A young boy had witnessed the entire incident. He had curiously approached the sage's hut after seeing the king's horse nearby. When the king left, the boy ran to his friends to tell them what had happened. Among the youths was the sage's son, Shringi. Infuriated by the insult afforded to his father,

Shringi, breathing heavily, criticised the king with harsh words.

"My father, the great sage Shamika, has been insulted by a low class member of the administrative caste! How could that lowly king have dared do such a thing?"

With furrowed brow, the immature boy, proud of his status as a sage's son, declared that kshatriyas were always meant to serve the brahmins.

"Just see the sinful behaviour of the so-called royal order. They should not even enter a brahmin's house uninvited. They are merely watchdogs and as such should remain obediently at the door. The king has severely transgressed religious principles."

Shringi had been educated by his father and knew the religious codes. In the symbolic societal body, brahmins were compared to the head, and the rulers or kshatriyas were the protective arms.

"It seems that since the departure of Lord Krishna, the upstart kings have forgotten their position," Shringi said. "Well, I shall deal with this matter myself."

By his birth and training, Shringi had the power to deliver curses. His eyes blazing red in self-righteous fury, he uttered an imprecation.

"On the seventh day from today, a snake bird will bite the wretch of a king, Parikit, due to his breaking the laws of etiquette by insulting my father!"

As he thundered out these words, Shringi touched the sacred waters of the nearby River Kaushiki, but even as he finished speaking, he at once felt remorse. What would his father say? The boy had never seen him display anger toward anyone. Would he have cursed the king in such a way? He ran toward his father's hut to tell him what he had done.

As Shringi entered the hermitage, he saw his father still sitting in silent meditation with the snake around his shoulders. The sight compounded his sorrow arising from regret and he cried out loudly. Hearing him wail in this way, Shamika slowly opened his eyes. Seeing the dead snake around his neck, he nonchalantly threw it aside and asked his son what was troubling him.

Trying to justify himself, Shringi explained, "Dear father, you were grievously insulted by Parikit with that snake. I have therefore cursed him to die in seven days."

Shamika's mouth fell open and his eyes opened wide. "What have you done? Such a king should never be cursed! Alas! You have awarded heavy punishment for an insignificant offence."

Shringi hung his head in shame as his father went on. "My boy, you are inexperienced. You do not know that the king is never to be considered an ordinary man. He is God's representative and therefore has the right to punish as he sees fit. The state prospers and remains peaceful only due to the prowess of a capable king like Parikit. By killing him, you will leave the world vulnerable to every kind of criminal. People will be killed and injured, women violated, animals harmed. Complete chaos will ensue. For all this we, the brahmins, will be to blame."

Shringi said nothing. He knew he was at fault. His father had many times instructed him in the importance of controlling anger.

Shamika continued. "Emperor Parikit is a pious and celebrated king. He is a great patron of religion and a man of staunch faith in the Supreme. When such a person is stricken with thirst and fatigue and then neglected, he does not at all deserve to be cursed."

Shamika knew Parikit would not retaliate against the wrong done to him. Krishna's devotees were so forbearing that even when defamed, cheated, cursed, or attacked, they are never inclined to avenge themselves. Still, the sage feared the Lord's displeasure for the offence against his devotee. The karmic reaction for cursing a great personality like Parikit would afflict the entire brahminical order, causing them to fall from their high principles. If that happened, then society would be ruined. Gradually the world would become like hell. The sage prayed to Krishna to forgive his thoughtless son.

19
Shukadeva Goswami Appears

Parikit leaves his kingdom to pursue self-realisation and meets Shukadeva Goswami, whom he questions as to the best course of action for one about to die.

(19:1-7) As Parikit entered his palace, he repeatedly castigated himself. Surely, he was uncivilised and impious. Summoning his ministers to the court, he described to them all that had happened. In anguish, he concluded, "Oh, what a wretch I am. Let my kingdom, wealth and opulence be burned up in the fire of the sage's wrath so that I not again commit such sin."

Trying to reassure the king, one minister suggested that since the sage would not know who had garlanded him with the snake, maybe there would be no consequence.

Parikit shook his head. "In my heart I know I will receive a severe reaction. Better it comes soon, for then I shall be free from the burden of sin and the possibility of committing another grievous offence."

Other advisors suggested that if he were sure the sage would know he was the wrongdoer, he should immediately return to the hermitage and beg for his forgiveness. "Your offense was not great. Surely he will excuse you."

Parikit was confused. He sat with his head in his hands. If only the wise Kripacharya was still with him. Just then a disciple of Shamika arrived at the palace. After informing Parikit about Shringi's curse, he said, "O king, when he learned of the curse made by his ignorant son, Sage Shamika scolded the boy. Not seeing any solution, he has fallen into grief. With a sorrowful heart, he has sent me to advise you to make necessary preparations for your soul's progressive journey."

When the disciple departed, Parikit turned to his counsellors and said, "I do not think it wise to now seek the sage's forgiveness. By so doing, I may simply embarrass him further. I do not even desire to negate the curse, which I consider most beneficial. I am now inclined to give up my material attachments. Indeed, it is my firm determination to completely fast as of this moment. Kindly make arrangements to enthrone my son, Janamejaya. I shall immediately proceed to the Yamuna's bank and there concentrate my mind on Lord Krishna."

The ministers cried out in sorrow and tried to dissuade Parikit, but he was resolute. Discarding his royal robes, and covering himself with a single cloth, he left his palace accompanied by brahmins. No one recognized him, thinking him to be an ascetic. Walking barefoot, and carrying a staff, he headed out of the city toward the River Ganges. He arrived mid-afternoon and after bathing in the sanctified waters, seated himself on the soft sandy bank, intending to remain there until his death.

(19:8-12) In a short time, thousands of sages along with their disciples, as well as many celestials and saintly kings also came to that place. They had heard of the curse and desiring the king's good had hurried to assist him prepare for death. Parikit recognised many of them, as they had previously visited his palace at the time of religious rituals. He had often performed great ceremonies which even the gods attended. He recognized among the gathered assembly, personalities including Atri, Vasishta, Vishvamitra, Vyasa, Maitreya, Parashurama, and even the great Narada Rishi. Parikit received them all by bowing his head to the ground. After the august visitors seated themselves around him, King Parikit stood before them with folded hands, and told them of his decision to fast to death.

(19:13-15) He said, "I am extremely grateful to you all for coming, as I know that generally, you great souls consider worldly kings like myself, to be like refuse, fit only to be rejected and left in a distant place."

The river flowed gently by, its rippling currents sparkling in the afternoon sun. White swans moved among the reeds and cranes stood in the shallows, watching for fish. The cries of birds and other forest creatures could be heard as the king continued to speak.

"The Supreme Lord has graciously overtaken me in the form of a brahmin's curse. Knowing me to be too attached to worldly possessions, he has appeared in such a way that out of fear alone, I will detach myself from the world. O great ones who know everything, I take full shelter of you and of this sacred River Ganges. I have already surrendered fully to the Lord in my heart. Let the snakebird—or whatever magical thing the brahmin conjured—bite me at once. I only desire to hear about the Supreme Lord's divine acts. Please therefore recite those to me."

(19:16-24) Once again offering prostrate obeisance to the sages, Parikit prayed, "Please bless me that even if I again take another material birth, I may have unstinting devotion to Krishna, association with his devotees, and friendly relations with all living beings."

From the heavens the gods showered him with flowers and beat celestial drums. The sages were also pleased, and they praised Parikit, saying, "Excellent! Very good!"

One of the sages stood up to speak on their behalf, saying, "O saintly king, it is not surprising that you have such determination to achieve Krishna's eternal association, coming as you do in the line of the Pandavas. We have all come to assist you."

Parikit bowed his head in humility. Feeling insignificant amidst so many exalted personalities, he said, "My dear sages, you have kindly assembled here, coming from all parts of the universe. Every one of you is as good as Lord Brahma, who is supreme knowledge personified. You have no business in this world other than benefiting others. I now ask you about my immediate duty. After proper deliberation, please also tell me the responsibility of one about to die."

Vyasadeva, Narada and other senior sages sat to the back and listened as various sages advised the king. One lean brahmin stood and spoke. "Your determination to attain Krishna's eternal abode is commendable. Yet, by abandoning your God-given duties you have acted against your own best interest."

A bearded hermit, wizened by long austerities, said, "Renouncing duties to pursue a life of ascetic meditation is always auspicious. You have done well,

147

my dear king, to leave your family and prosperous kingdom."

Still another mendicant spoke. "Both of you venerable ones speak wisely. However, the king wanted advice specific to himself. He has only one week left to live. He does not have sufficient time to successfully execute all the vows of a mendicant. Maybe he would do better to continue to rule his kingdom until his last moment."

A debate began among the sages. Should the king follow the path of ascetic renunciation or adhere to his kingly duties? Listening to them, Parikit felt disheartened. These debates could take much time to resolve, but he only had seven days to perfect his life.

(19:25-40) At that moment he heard a commotion coming from behind him. All the sages stopped talking and rose up with respect. Turning around, Parikit saw a naked youth walking toward him, surrounded by a throng of women and children, all jeering. The young man remained peaceful, undisturbed by their derision.

The newcomer was strikingly handsome. His complexion was dark like Krishna's; his eyes were wide, and his nose raised. Curls of blackish hair fell around his smiling face. His limbs were long and finely formed, and his movements graceful. The sages, recognising him as Vyasadeva's son, warmly greeted him. "Welcome Shukadeva Goswami! We are blessed by your presence!"

Shukadeva returned their greetings by embracing some, shaking hands with others, and bowing down to his respected elders, including Vyasadeva and Narada, who had remained seated. Parikit bowed his head in respect as Shukadeva took his place among the sages. The women and children who had been mocking him were astonished, and they quickly dispersed. Sitting among the other sages, Shukadeva looked like the moon surrounded by stars and planets.

Parikit had previously heard of Vyasadeva's exalted son. It was said he never mixed with worldly people longer than it took to milk a cow, preferring to remain absorbed in spiritual trance. Understanding the great favour Shukadeva was bestowing on him by coming at this difficult time in his life, Parikit meekly greeted him.

"My dear sir, we are sanctified by your presence, which transforms everywhere you go into a holy place of pilgrimage. It is by your mercy alone that I am able to see you today in my hour of greatest need. By simply remembering you, a man becomes purified of sin. Surely it is due only to my relationship with the Pandavas, who are so dear to Krishna, that the Lord has favoured me by sending you, the spiritual master even for great saints. I therefore beg you to show the way of perfection for all people, and especially for one about to die."

Smiling, Shukadeva began to reply.

End of Canto One

Appendix 1

Chapter 2, text 17 describes *anisthita* bhakti, or unsteady devotional service. In Madhyura Kadambini, Vishvanatha Cakravarti Thakura gives more information about this stage as follows:

"Anisthita (unsteady devotional service) is further divided into six gradations:

utsahamayi (sudden enthusiasm)

ghana-tarala (sometimes enthusiastic, sometimes lethargic)

vyudha-vikalpa (a stage when doubts assail one's resolve)

visaya-sangara (a stage of internal tug-of-war with material sense enjoyment)

niyamaksama (although one practises regularly, full justice is still not done to the process)

taranga-rangini (attachment to wealth, adoration, distinction, and so on).

Let us first discuss the beginning stage of bhajana-kriya -- the stage of utsahamayi. When a young student begins higher education, he is very proud, thinking himself to be a praiseworthy scholar. Such thoughts encourage the student to apply himself and to perform well. Similarly, when a novice commences spiritual life, he takes to it so enthusiastically, thinking himself to be somebody special.

The example of the same young scholar explains the stage of ghana-tarala. At times the student concentrates deeply on his studies, but sometimes, because of his inability to understand something, he becomes apathetic. In devotional activities the neophyte goes through similar spells of opposing attitudes sometimes enthusiasm, other times lethargy.

Vyudha-vikalpa is an interesting stage on the path of spiritual life. sometimes the devotee thinks "I shall convince my wife and family to become Vaishnavas and serve the Supreme Lord. I shall convert my house into a temple and remain there happily practicing devotional service." At other times he thinks, "I shall leave my family, home, and the rest of my worries behind me and go to Vrindavana. I shall reside there, for it is the holiest of places, and I shall cultivate devotional surrender through the nine practices of devotion." Or he will say, "Ultimately, I have to give up my home and all my other attachments, then should I not first plunge into the pool of sensual pleasures until I am satisfied?"

Or he may think, "The scriptures speak of family and wife being like a dark and dismal well. Should I not leave home this very moment? Sometimes the scriptures encourage me to perceive that this material life, family connections, wife, children are abominable and to renounce them. Yet how can I do that? My parents are old and infirm, who will take care of them? Besides, if I should leave home prematurely, with my material desires to enjoy still unfulfilled, my mind will continue to dwell on sense pleasures until my final days. This would be a disaster! Therefore, I can understand from my own thoughts that I am too weak to follow the Lord's instructions and renounce family life. For now I shall live simply. When the proper time comes I shall hasten to Vrndavana and spend my days and nights in deep meditation on the pastimes of the Supreme Lord."

The scriptures (SB. 11.20.31) say that neither knowledge nor renunciation is helpful in performing devotional service; since renunciation cannot give birth to bhakti, practicing renunciation separately is unnecessary. After one is situated in devotional service, however, renunciation is an asset because then renunciation proves not only the effectiveness of bhakti but also its superiority. it is both wrong and foolish to cultivate knowledge and renunciation separately once a person enters the path of devotional service.

A famous aphorism in logic is, "When the renunciate goes begging from door-to-door, he finds all the family larders full with grains because he is given charity." Basing his argument on this logic the aspiring devotee thinks, "I must take up renunciation". Next moment he comes across another scriptural maxim (SB.10.14.36) stating that unless one develops loving devotion to the Lord his home is a prison. So he says to himself, "Must I remain in household life and try to develop devotional surrender to the Lord? Maybe I should practice hearing about Krsna or chanting Krsna's name and fame. Should I emulate Ambarisa Maharaja and simultaneously perform all the nine devotional activities?" When bhajana-kriya goes through this state of doubt and vacillating resolve it is known as vyudha-vikalpa.

Visaya-sangara is the stage when conflicting doubts and arguments are resolved in the devotee's heart and he is convinced about the path of renunciation. Scripture states that just as an object lost in the west cannot be found in the east, similarly, a person engrossed in materialistic activities will never become attached to Krsna. The devotee feels that his desires for sensual enjoyment are forcing him towards fulfilling them, and so his attraction for chanting and devotional service becomes weak. Therefore he thinks he should immediately discard those desires and wholeheartedly chant the holy name, although even in the process he may sometimes fall victim to sense gratification. The devotee still remains convinced of the scriptural truth that perfection can be achieved through devotional service. And although he may fall prey to sense enjoyment, he rebukes himself and feels remorseful, always continuing his devotional practices. Thus the devotee wages a war against his desire for sense gratification: sometimes the victor, sometimes the defeated. When he does fall victim, the devotee at this stage of unsteady devotional service still feels regret and revulsion at his weakness.

The next stage of unsteady devotional service is niyamaksama, where the devotee vows to increase his devotional activities. He resolves to chant sixty-four rounds daily, offer one hundred prostrated obeisances to the Deities and the Vaisnavas; serve the senior devotees; avoid talking about mundane topics; shun the company of materialistic minded people, and so on. Daily he makes these vows, but at the last moment he is unable to honor them. The difference between visayasangara and niyamaksama is that in the former the devotee is helpless to give up material sense pleasures, and in the latter he is unable to increase and improve his devotional activities.

Now let us discuss taranga-rangini the last stage of anisthita devotional service. In describing the nature of bhakti it is said that everyone is attracted towards the reservoir of bhakti, the devotee. The devotee himself becomes a treasure-house of good qualities and mercy. These characteristics attract people who, in turn, crown the devotee with wealth, adoration, distinction and position. Although these accolades come to him as by-products of bhakti they nevertheless may stunt the spontaneous growth of the creeper of devotion if he uses them for his self-aggrandizement. Taranga means "waves" and rangini means "play". Therefore, in the vast unlimited ocean of bhakti these by-products are waves that create tempests in devotional life. The devotee aspiring for pure devotion sees these waves to be harmless,-only gleefully playing and cresting." *Madhurya Kadambini* 3: The Third Shower of Nectar

Appendix 2

In Madhyura Kadambini, Vishvanatha Chakravarti Thakur explains what is meant by the unwanted things in the heart being almost gone as follows:

1. What is troublesome to the heart: "(Anartha means unwanted desires in the heart, and nivrtti means to cease.) There are four kinds of anartha:

(1) Duskrtottha (anarthas coming from sinful activities)

(2) Sukrtottha (anarthas coming from pious deeds)

(3) Aparadhottha (anarthas coming from offences)

(4) Bhaktyuttha (anarthas coming from devotional service)

Earlier we discussed the bad effects of material attachments, such as envy and anger. These causes of distress are born of sinful activities (duskrti). The craving for temporary sensual pleasure is also a detrimental desire in the heart, an anartha stemming from sukrti (pious activities). [Suffering comes from impious deeds, whereas pious deeds facilitate enjoyment of the senses.] Some scholars say that sukrtottha anarthas are part of the five causes of distress: envy, pride, anger, ignorance, and attachment." *Third shower pages*

2. Stages of removal of the above anarthas:

"Now we shall talk further on the anarthas (unwanted desires) that crop up in the execution of devotional service. Unwanted desires tend to smother the natural growth of the creeper of bhakti. At first glance unwanted desires look like off-shoots from the bhakti-lata (the creeper of devotion), but in reality they are mundane desires for position, adoration, and opulence. They color and taint the practitioner's consciousness. Thriving in this way these anarthas arrest the growth of the creeper of devotional service.

The four anarthas mentioned in the beginning of this chapter can be mitigated in the five following ways:

i) eka-desavarttini (partially)

ii) bahu-desavarttini (substantially)

iii) prayiki (almost completely)

iv) purna (completely)

v) atyantiki (absolutely thoroughly).

The many anarthas stemming from aparadhas are partially destroyed in the final stages of bhajana-kriya (rendering devotional service under the guidance of a spiritual master). This is known as eka-desavarttini. **When bhajana-kriya gains maturity it turns to nistha, or steadiness, in devotional activities. In this stage of development, the mitigation of anarthas is substantial (bahu-desavarttini);** thereafter, on the platform of rati (attraction) the unwanted desires in the heart are almost completely absolved (prayiki). With the first awakening of prema, or divine love, these anarthas are completely removed (purna). Finally, the anarthas are totally uprooted (atyantiki) when the devotee receives the mercy and shelter of the Lord's lotus feet." *Third Shower*

Summary of the above by the authors: there are four categories of unwanted desires in the heart of the aspiring devotee. These are as follows:

1. Unwanted desires generated by our past sinful activities;
2. Unwanted desires generated by our past pious activities;
3. Unwanted desires generated by our offences;
4. Unwanted desires generated by performing sadhana bhakti.

When one becomes steady in his devotional practises, all these unwanted desires are substantially cleared.

Appendix 3

These verses describe the 9 stages of advancement from initial faith in Krishna to the awakening of divine love. The nine stages are summarized by Rupa Goswami in the following stanza: *adau sraddha tatah sadhu- sango 'tha bhajana-kriyatato 'nartha-nivrttih syat tato nistha rucis tatahathasaktis tato bhavas tatah premabhyudancati sadhakanam ayam premnah pradurbhave bhavet kramah,* 'In the beginning there must be faith. Then one becomes interested in associating with pure devotees. Thereafter one is initiated by the spiritual master and executes the regulative principles under his orders. Thus, one is freed from all unwanted habits and becomes firmly fixed in devotional service. Thereafter, one develops taste and attachment. This is the way of sadhana-bhakti, the execution of devotional service according to the regulative principles. Gradually emotions intensify, and finally there is an awakening of love. This is the gradual development of love of Godhead for the devotee interested in Krsna consciousness.' *Caitanya Caritamrita Madhya 23.14–15*

Srila Prabhupada explains these stages as follows:

"The first stage is sraddha, a little faith. Just like our students are going in the marketplace, they are chanting, and many people are contributing some money, somebody's purchasing our Back to Godhead. This is the beginning of faith: "Oh, here is a nice movement. Let me cooperate." Adau sraddha.
Then, if he becomes little more interested, then he comes here, into the class: "All right, let us see what

these people are teaching, this Krsna consciousness." So they come. So that is the second stage. The first stage is automatic sympathy for this movement. The second stage is joining or associating with this, our activities. Just like you have kindly come here. You are hearing me. Similarly, if somebody becomes more interested or his faith is still further advanced, then he comes, that is the second stage.

And the third stage is... Adau sraddha tatah sadhu-sanga atha bhajana-kriya [Cc. Madhya 23.14]. [In the beginning there must be faith. Then one becomes interested in associating with pure devotees. Thereafter one is initiated by the spiritual master and executes the regulative principles under his orders. Thus one is freed from all unwanted habits and becomes firmly fixed in devotional service. Thereafter, one develops taste and attachment. This is the way of sadhana-bhakti, the execution of devotional service according to the regulative principles. Gradually emotions intensify, and finally there is an awakening of love. This is the gradual development of love of Godhead for the devotee interested in Krsna consciousness.]

Now, the initiation means beginning of the activities. Beginning of the activities. How one can develop Krsna consciousness to the perfectional state, that is called initiation. It is not that initiation means finished. It is the third stage. Then the fourth stage will be, one who is initiated, if he follows the rules and regulation, and if he chants Hare Krsna with a fixed-up counting, then gradually his all misgivings will vanish. What are the misgivings? We ask our students to refrain from that illicit sex life, nonvegetarian diet, and intoxication, and to take [sic] part in gambling. These four things. So ordinarily these four things are very prominent in the society, especially in the Western

159

countries. But these students who take initiation and follows chanting, they very easily give up these four things without any difficulty. That is called anartha nivrtti. That is the fourth stage.

The fifth stage is then he becomes fixed up: "Yes." Just like one student, Mr. Anderson, I've not seen him, but simply by associating with our other devotees, he has written that "I wish to devote my whole being for this Krsna consciousness." This is called nistha, fixed up. Tato nistha tato ruci. Ruci means they get a taste. Why these boys are going out? This chanting, they have got a taste. They have developed a taste. Otherwise for nothing they are not wasting time. They are educated, they are grown up. So taste. Fixed up, then taste, tathasaktis. When the taste is, then attachment. He cannot give it up.

And I receive so many letters. Some students, they could not cope with their Godbrothers, they go away, but they'll write that "I cannot go. I cannot go." He's captured. You see? [chuckles] Umapati has written that letter, that he becomes in difficulty, he cannot live..., he cannot l-i-v-e or l-e-a-v-e. He's in Dallas. You see?

He cannot quit the company, or some misunderstanding, he cannot live with Godbrothers. But that is temporary. So that is called asaktih, attachment. Tathasaktis tato bhava. Then gradually increasing, some ecstatic position, always thinking of Krsna. And then perfectional stage, that he loves Krsna cent per cent. So this is the process." *Lecture & Initiation -- October 20, 1968, Seattle*

Notes

SB= Srimad Bhagavatam, translated by Srila Prabhupada

Bg = Bhagavad-gita As It Is, translated by Srila Prabhupada

1. "The goal of life in the material world, ...(is) generally: religiosity, economic development, sense gratification and liberation. Dharma, artha, kama, moksa." *Srila Prabhupada Lecture -- March 12, 1975, London*; "The fruitive workers, the salvationists, and also the yogis who are after mystic powers are all unhappy because of unfulfilled desires." *Bg 2.70 purport*

2. Note: "There are different kinds of activities -- karma, jnana, yoga, especially. Everything, all activities, are grouped under three headings." *Lecture on Bhagavad-gita 4.39–42 -- January 14, 1969, Los Angeles.*

3. "The principles of bhakti-yoga-sravanam kirtanam visnoh smaranam pada-sevanam/ arcanam vandanam dasyam sakhyam atma-nivedanam [SB 7.5.23] -- are the only means by which perfection can be attained. Simply by hearing of the glories of the Lord, one is elevated to the transcendental position." *SB 4.29.39–40*

4. "Occupational duties are known as varnasrama-dharma and apply to the four divisions of material and spiritual life -- namely brahmana, ksatriya, vaisya and sudra, and brahmacarya, grhastha, vanaprastha and sannyasa." *4.20.9 purport*; "Varnasrama-dharma is called dharma." *Lecture on Srimad-Bhagavatam 7.6.4 -- December 5, 1975, Vrndavana.*

5. "The word dharma means 'duty.' Although the word dharma is often translated as "religion" and religion is generally defined as a kind of faith, dharma is not in fact a kind of faith. Dharma means one's actual constitutional duty. It is one's duty to know the needs of the soul, but unfortunately we have no information of the soul and are simply busy supplying the necessities for bodily comfort." Teachings of Queen Kunti Note: "One has therefore to learn from Krsna directly or from a pure devotee of Krsna -- and not from a nondevotee upstart, puffed up with academic education." *Bg 7.1 purport.*

6. "As one associates with pure devotees and hears them submissively, attachment for material enjoyment slackens and attraction for hearing about the transcendental activities of the Lord becomes prominent. Once this attraction begins, it goes on progressively increasing without stoppage, like fire in gunpowder." *SB 1.10.11-12 purport*

7. "The purpose of dharma-artha-kama-moksa means to come to this platform of bhakti. The Bhagavata says that.. 'The occupational activities a man performs according to his own position are only so much useless labor if they do not provoke attraction for the message of the Personality of Godhead.' (SB 1.2.8)

"The purpose of dharma artha kama is to come to the platform of bhakti. If one does not come to that platform, simply as a matter of formula and rituals, the Bhagavata says it is simply waste of time." *Lecture on Srimad-Bhagavatam 7.9.9 -- July 6, 1968, Montreal.*

8. "Oneness with the impersonal brahma-jyoti is not ultimate liberation; superior to that is the sublime association of the Personality of Godhead in one of the innumerable spiritual planets in the Vaikuntha sky." *SB 2.5.16 purport*

9. "Any person who desires the fruits of the four

principles religiosity, economic development, sense gratification and, at the end, liberation, should engage himself in the devotional service of the Supreme Personality of Godhead, for worship of His lotus feet yields the fulfillment of all of these." *SB 4.8.41 verse*

10. "By following the principles of the varnasrama-dharma, one attains a better position in the material world. One may be rich, learned, beautiful or highborn. One who has all these assets should know that **they are all meant for the advancement of Krsna consciousness**. Unfortunately, when a person is misguided he misuses his high position for sense gratification. Therefore the uncontrolled senses are considered plunderers. The good position one attains by executing religious principles is wasted as the plundering senses take it away. By executing religious principles under the laws of varnasrama-dharma, one is placed in a comfortable position. One may very easily use his assets for the further advancement of Krsna consciousness. One should understand that the wealth and opportunity one gets in the material world should not be squandered in sense gratification. They are meant for the advancement of Krsna consciousness." *SB 5.14.2 purport*

11. "Lord Brahma said, 'My dear Lord, those devotees who have thrown away the impersonal conception of the Absolute Truth and have therefore abandoned discussing empiric philosophical truths **should hear from self-realized devotees** about Your holy name, form, pastimes and qualities." *Caitanya Caritamrita, Madhya Lila 8.67 verse*.

12. "Lord Brahma said, 'My dear Lord, those devotees who have thrown away the impersonal conception of the Absolute Truth and have therefore abandoned discussing empiric philosophical truths **should hear from self-realized devotees** about Your holy name,

form, pastimes and qualities." Caitanya Caritamrita, Madhya Lila 8.67 verse

13."Prema-bhakti is the stage of spontaneous love of Godhead, whereas sadhana-bhakti means the conscientious practice of the regulative principles of devotional service." SB 11.7.11 purport

14. "If one reads Bhagavad-gita very sincerely and with all seriousness, then by the grace of the Lord the reactions of his past misdeeds will not act upon him." (Gita-mahatmya 2) The Lord says very loudly in the last portion of Bhagavad-gita (18.66)...."Abandon all varieties of religion and just surrender unto Me. I shall deliver you from all sinful reactions. Do not fear." Thus the Lord takes all responsibility for one who surrenders unto Him, and He indemnifies such a person against all reactions of sins." Bhagavad gita As It Is; Introduction.

15. "Thus Narottama dasa Thakura says, chadiya vaisnava-seva nistara payeche keba: without serving a pure devotee, one cannot advance in spiritual life. ...One should take shelter of a pure devotee, who has nothing to do with this material world but is simply engaged in devotional service. By serving him only, one can transcend the qualitative material condition. In this verse it is recommended (yogesvara-upasanaya) that one serve the lotus feet of the topmost yogi, or the devotee. To serve the topmost devotee means to hear from him about the glories of the Supreme Personality of Godhead. To hear the glories of the Supreme Personality of Godhead from the mouth of a pure devotee is to acquire a pious life." SB 4.22.22 purport.

16. According to Visvanatha Cakravarti Thakura in Madhyura Kadambini, verse 17 describes unsteady devotional service, and verse 18 describes steady devotional service. *"srnvatam sva-kathah krsnah*

punya-sravana-kirtanah hrdy antah-stho hy abhadrani vidhunoti suhrt satam 'Sri Krsna, the Personality of Godhead, who is the Paramatma [Supersoul] in everyone's heart and the benefactor of the truthful devotee, cleanses desire for material enjoyment from the heart of the devotee who has developed the urge to hear His messages, which are in themselves virtuous when properly heard and chanted.' *nasta-prayesv abhadresu nityam bhagavata-sevaya bhagavaty uttama-sloke bhaktir bhavati naisthiki* 'By regular attendance in classes on the Bhagavatam and by rendering of service to the pure devotee, all that is troublesome to the heart is almost completely destroyed, and loving service unto the Personality of Godhead, who is praised with transcendental songs, is established as an irrevocable fact.' The Supreme Lord is the greatest benefactor of the pure devotees, the saintly sadhus. Therefore the only way to receive the Lord's mercy is to first receive the grace of the pure devotees. The first verse quoted previously describes the unsteady *bhajana-kriya* stage of devotional service. The second verse (1.2.18) describes *naisthiki-*bhakti, or steady devotional service, also known as the *nistha* stage. In describing the two stages of bhakti both the verses mention destroying inauspicious things in the heart, of purifying the heart of unwanted material desires. The second verse quoted suites that impurities are almost completely destroyed, meaning that some residue of impurity is still there in the heart." *Madhurya Kadambini 4: The Fourth Shower of Nectar*

17. "When naisthiki-bhakti blossoms in the devotee's consciousness, the immediate effect is that he is no longer ruled by anger, greed, or any other influences from the modes of passion and ignorance. The naisthiki bhakta becomes firmly fixed on the Supreme

Lord, who is always situated in pure goodness, and experiences divine bliss. The Srimad-Bhagavatam (1.2.19) confirms this: tada rajas-tamo-bhavah kama-lobhadayas ca ye ceta etair anaviddham sthitam sattve prasidati, *'As soon as irrevocable loving service is established in the heart the effects of nature's modes of passion and ignorance, such as lust, desire and hankering, disappear from the heart. Then the devotee is established in goodness, and he becomes completely happy.'*

In this verse, the Sanskrit word ca ("and") conveys the presence of passion and ignorance in the heart of the devotee. But in the same verse the expression ceta etair anaviddham (that the mind is unaffected by these) establishes that these material modes are not obstacles on the path of devotion, but reside in the heart in a neutral state until the devotee on the platform of steady devotional service attains bhava. (Bhava is the stage of spontaneous loving devotion to the Lord.)" *Madhurya Kadambini*: Fourth Shower

18. "This means that by lack of taste for material objects, the state of ruci—the appearance of relishing of hearing, chanting and other processes—arises. In the previous state, the mind was pierced by the sharp arrows of lust and greed etc. How could the mind be satisfied in that state? How could the mind attain a real taste for chanting in that state?" *Vishvanatha Chakravarti Thakur's commentary on SB 1.2.19*.

19. Note: See Bg 18.54.

20. "After this, the mind becomes fixed (*sthitam*) in the shuddha-sattva deity of the Lord (sattve). This is the stage of ashakti." *Vishvanatha Chakravarti Thakur's commentary to SB 1.2.19*

21. "In the seed of affection, there is attachment which goes by two names, rati and bhava." *Caitanya Caritamrita, Madhya 22.165 verse*

22. "Then the mind becomes joyful and satisfied on attaining rati. Finally prema develops..." *Vishvanatha Chakravarti Thakura's commentary on SB 1.2.20*

23. "With the first awakening of prema, or divine love, these anarthas are completely removed (purna). Finally, the anarthas are totally uprooted (atyantiki) when the devotee receives the mercy and shelter of the Lord's lotus feet." Vishvanatha Chakravarti's Madhyura Kadambini: Third Shower.

24. In connection with the Virat Rupa being imaginary, VCT explains in his commentary on this verse (1.3.30) that the conditioned souls' material bodies are also imaginary in the same way. We therefore understand that the Virat Rupa is a real material form, not just a convention applied to the planets. Srila Prabhupada also explains in the purport how it is imaginary: "As Paramatma, or Supersoul, the Lord is within each and every material form, even within the atoms, but the outward material form is but an imagination, both for the Lord and for the living being. The present forms of the conditioned souls are also not factual. The conclusion is that the material conception of the body of the Lord as *virat* is imaginary. Both the Lord and the living beings are living spirits and have original spiritual bodies."

25. Tattva Sandarbha by Jiva Goswami. Anuccheda 49

26. "Wearing a peacock-feather ornament upon his head, blue karnikara flowers on his ears, a yellow garment as brilliant as gold, and his divine Vaijayanti garland, Lord Krishna exhibited his transcendental form as the greatest dancer as he entered the forest of Vrndavana, beautifying it with his footprints. He filled the holes of his flute with the nectar of his lips, and the cowherd boys sang his glories" *Srimad Bhagavatam 10.21.5.*

27. Additional details of this and other episodes

concerning the Pandavas are taken from *Mahabharata: The Greatest Spiritual Epic of all Time* by Krishna Dharma.

28. "The subject matter which attracts the dying man becomes the beginning of his next life." (*Srimad Bhagavatam* 1.9.30 purport by Srila Prabhupada) "The eagerness to hear about God is the first qualification of a devotee eligible for entering the kingdom of God." (*Srimad Bhagavatam* 1.2.16 purport by Srila Prabhupada)

29. Nectar of Devotion Chapter 22 (Bhaktivedanta Book Trust)

30. Bhagavad-gita

GLOSSARY

Agni: God of fire, thus also the Sanskrit word for fire.

Anartha: Literally 'unwanted' – impurity of the heart.

Apsara: Celestial nymph of legendary beauty.

Arati: Worship ceremony in which articles like incense, flowers, and fans are offered.

Arghya: Milk-based drink used as a respectful offering made to a guest.

Astra: Divine weapon, usually prefixed by the name of the particular god or force which presides over it; e.g. Brahmastra, a weapon presided over by Lord Brahma.

Asura: Persons possessed of atheistic mentality.

Avadhuta: A saint with no affiliation or attachment to anything material.

Avatar: Appearance of a form of Vishnu within the material world.

Bhairava: Name for Shiva.

Bhava: First stage of love of God.

Brahma: First of the gods and the creator of the universe.

Brahman: The absolute supreme spiritual reality. Krishna's energy.

Brahmana: The priestly class, usually teachers.

Brihaspati: The gods' preceptor.

Chamara: Whisk made from yak-tail hairs and used for highly respectable persons.

Charana: Class of celestials noted for their poetic abilities.

Daitya: Class of powerful demonic beings.

Danava: Class of powerful celestial demons who are the gods' enemies.

Devi: Goddess. Also used as respectful term of address for one's wife.

Dwapara-yuga: Third of the four Vedic ages

Gandharva: Celestial beings famed for their singing and dancing ability, as well as their prowess in battle.

Gandiva: Arjuna's bow.

Garbhodaka: Great ocean filling half of the universe in which lies Garbhodakashayi Vishnu.

Garbhodakashayi Vishnu: Second *Purusha* Avatar or functional incarnation of Vishnu who enters each material universe to facilitate creation.

Gopa: Cowherd man.

Gopi: Cowherd woman.

Indra: King of the gods, also known as Purandara and Shakra.

Japa: Chanting of God's names.

Jaya: Victory or 'All glories'. An exclamation of approval and appreciation.

Jiva: Soul in the material world.

Kali-yuga: Last of the four Vedic ages, also known as the Age of Quarrel and Hypocrisy.

Kalpa: One day of Lord Brahma, or 1000 cycles of the four ages on earth.

Karanodakashayi Vishnu: First *Purusha* Avatar or functional incarnation of Vishnu, also known as Mahavishnu, from whom the universes emanate.

Kauravas: Sons of Dhritarastra.

Kinnara: A class of god, often having a half-human and half- animal form such as that of a centaur, and generally seen holding a lute.

Kirtan: Glorification of Krishna.

Kshatriya: Member of the administrative or ruling class, usually warriors. Considered subordinate to *brahmanas.*

Kshirodakashayi Vishnu: Third *Purusha* Avatar or function incarnation of Vishnu who acts as the Supersoul.

Kusha: *Darbha* grass, considered sacred by the

Vedas.

Kuvera: God of wealth, who guards the northern quarter of the universe.

Lokapalas: Gods presiding over the four quarters of the universe.

Mahat-tattva: The total material elements in their non-manifest form.

Makara: Legendary sea creature resembling a huge shark with a crocodile's head.

Maya Danava: A celestial demon possessing great skills at architecture and building.

Manu: Incarnation of Vishnu who rules over mankind.

Naga: Celestial serpent, often appearing in human form.

Naimisharanya: Sacred forest said to be the 'hub' of the universe.

Narada: A celestial sage also known as Devarshi, or the sage among the gods.

Narayana: Name for Vishnu.

Nishadha: Tribal people living in the forest.

Nishtha: Stage of steady practise in *sadhana bhakti*.

Pandavas: Sons of King Pandu.

Parashurama: A sage said to be an empowered incarnation of Vishnu.

Pranayama: A stage of yoga practise where one controls the breathing.

Prema: Pure love for Krishna.

Puranas: Vedic histories, compiled by Vyasadeva.

Rahu: A powerful demon appearing as a shadowy planet.

Rakshasa: Celestial demon, antagonistic to humankind.

Rama: Incarnation of Vishnu, who appeared as a king in the solar dynasty.

Rati: Taste for devotional practise.

Ravana: Powerful leader of the Rakshasa race.

Rishi: Sage.

Rudra: Name for Lord Shiva.

Sadhana: The practises of devotional service.

Sagara: King of the Solar Race. The ocean is also called *"sagara"* as it was the sons of this king who first excavated it.

Sanjivani: Mystical mantra that can bring the dead back to life.

Sankhya: Philosophical process of spiritual advancement which analyses reality.

Satya-yuga: First of the four Vedic ages, also known as the Golden Age.

Shiva: Partial expansion of Vishnu who acts as the universal destroyer at the end of a cycle of ages.

Siddha: Literally, a perfected being. Also a class of gods possessing great mystic powers.

Sita: The daughter of King Janaka who became Rama's wife.

Shudra: Member of the working class who assist the other three classes in society.

Surabhi: A type of celestial cow that gives anything one desires.

Swayamvara: Ceremony where a maiden chooses her own husband.

Timingila: Monstrous aquatic capable of swallowing a whale.

Treta-yuga: Second of the four Vedic ages.

Vaikuntha: The eternal spiritual world.

Vaishya: Member of the productive class, often agriculturalists.

Varna: Vocation.

Varnashrama: Vedic social system of four vocational and four spiritual divisions.

Varuna: God of the waters and the nether worlds.

Vedanta: Short codes compiled by Vyasadeva giving

the essence of Vedic knowledge.

Vedas: Ancient Sanskrit scriptures.

Vidhyadhara: A class of god.

Virat Rupa: Universal form of God.

Vishnu: Expansion of Krishna in his role as creator and maintainer of the material world.

Vishnurata: Name for Parikit meaning 'protected by Vishnu.'

Vishvarupa: Universal form of God

Yaksha: Class of gods who are servants of Kuvera.

Yamaduta: Yamaraja's messengers who bring him sinful persons after they die.

Yamaraja: The god who presides over death and destiny. He is empowered by Vishnu to award all beings the results of their actions. He guards the southern quarter of the universe.

Yuga: Vedic age, of which there are four.

Authors' Note

This is the first book in a series covering the entire
Srimad Bhagavatam. Readers interested in the
subject matter are welcome to contact us via the
website: www.krishnadharma.com, where they will
also find information about Krishna Dharma's other
books, writings and speaking engagements. We are
only too aware that this book may well contain errors
and omissions, and if you should note any, please let
us know so they can be corrected in future editions.
We also welcome questions which you can put to us
on Krishna Dharma's Facebook page:
https://www.facebook.com/krishnadharma.author/

Thank you for reading the book. We hope you
found it helpful. If so, we would be grateful if you
could write a review on Amazon or any other website
where you found the book.

OTHER TITLES IN THE SERIES.

Volume two: Mysteries of Creation

In this second canto of *Srimad Bhagavatam* we hear the great sage Shukadeva Goswami answering the questions of King Parikit, who has been cursed to die in seven days. After briefly delineating man's highest duty and the best way to conquer suffering and death, Shukadeva explains the path of mystic yoga and meditation. We are then introduced to Lord Brahma, greatest of the gods and engineer of the universe. Questioned by his son Narada, another powerful mystic, he describes the process of creation. We hear how the all-powerful Supreme Person manifests the elements from his spiritual body, enters them, and produces the template for creation which Brahma then effects. 'Mysteries of Creation' presents this profound and illuminating knowledge in a simplified and dramatic style, making it accessible to all.

Volume three: Vidura's Pilgrimage

In this third canto we travel with the saint Vidura, of *Mahabharata* fame, as he meets first with Uddhava, Krishna's secretary and close confidante, and then with the great sage Maitreya. We hear fascinating details about Krishna's divine pastimes, as well as revelations about the cosmos and the nature of time. Replete with powerful mystical teachings spoken by sages and gods, this insightful book will touch your heart and leave you feeling spiritually inspired and renewed.

Volume four: Two Avatars

The second part of canto three, in which we hear about the appearance of Vishnu's stupendous boar incarnation, Lord Varaha, who rescues the earth from the demon Hiranyaksha. We also meet the great sage Kardama, who marries Devahuti, daughter of the earth's emperor, Manu. She gives birth to Lord Kapila, the divine incarnation who descended to teach the ancient science of Sankhya Yoga. Filled with enlightening wisdom and stimulating stories, Two Avataras presents the ancient teachings of the epic Srimad Bhagavatam in a highly enjoyable way that will appeal to anyone seeking real peace and lasting happiness.

Volume five: Krishna Fulfils All Desires.

The whole of Srimad Bhagavatam Canto 4 where we hear the great sage Maitreya recounting the histories of a number of great saints, mystics and divine incarnations, which illustrate how the Lord awards us whatever we desire. Ultimately we learn that, in order to achieve complete happiness, we should only desire Krishna's loving service. We see how he expertly fulfills our desires in such a way that we will eventually come to this realization.

Made in United States
Troutdale, OR
07/06/2023

11018514R00106